JOHN
STARKS
MY LIFE

JOHN STARKS

With Dan Markowitz
Foreword by Spike Lee

www.SportsPublishingLLC.com

www.johnstarks.com

ISBN: 1-58261-802-X

Publisher: Peter L. Bannon
Senior managing editor: Susan M. Moyer
Acquisitions and developmental editor: Noah Amstadter
Book design and senior project manager: Jennifer L. Polson
Dust jacket and insert design: Joseph Brumleve
Imaging: Dustin Hubbart, Chris Mohrbacher and Heidi Norsen
Copy editor: Cynthia L. McNew
Photo editor: Erin Linden-Levy
Vice president of sales and marketing: Kevin King
Media and promotions managers: Jonathan Patterson (regional),
        Randy Fouts (national), Maurey Williams (print)

Printed in the United States of America

Sports Publishing L.L.C.
804 North Neil Street
Champaign, IL 61820

Phone: 1-877-424-2665
Fax: 217-363-2073
Web site: www.SportsPublishingLLC.com

In memory of my mother, Irene; grandmother, Callie West;
and sister Anita for being shining lights in my life.
May God rest their souls. Also to my brothers and sister
Nicole for being there when I needed you. Much love.
To my wife Jackie for having my back and my three beautiful
children: John Jr., Chelsea and my little princess Tiara.

–J.S.

To my mother, Selma, and Jeanne for their love,
support and guidance.
To Coach Allan Hubschman, my high school basketball coach
at Rye Neck, who taught me to respect the game of basketball.
To Walt Frazier, who made me love the game.

–D.M.

CONTENTS

FOREWORD
BY SPIKE LEE

The reason why I wore John Starks's New York Knicks No. 3 jersey when I sat courtside at Madison Square Garden was because he *was* the Knicks. Why do I say that? On a team that had a future Hall of Famer Patrick Ewing, Charles Oakley and several other excellent players, why the man from Tulsa, Oklahoma?

To me, Mr. Starks got more out of what he had—and from where he come from—than most human beings ever do. How does one go from packing bags at a grocery store not just to the NBA, but to become an NBA All-Star? You will find this book fascinating.

My fondest memory of John was probably the worst game in his professional career. This was the seventh and final game of the 1994 NBA Championships, Knicks vs. the Houston Rockets. As it's been well documented John shot two for 18, hence the Knicks lost. Only recently has then-Knicks coach Pat Riley finally admitted that he should have taken John out of the game to see if sharp-shooter Rolondo Blackmon could hit a shot.

After the game I went into the tomb-like Knicks dressing room. I was looking for John, to console him, give him a hug, to let him know that it was just one of those nights. He played hard as he did every time he stepped on the court, but tonight the shots wouldn't drop.

I went around the dressing room telling the guys thanks for a great year and hopefully we'll be back next year. After waiting for 30 minutes I asked one of the ball boys to see when John would be out. A few minutes later he came back and said John was still in the showers. I turned around and left the Knicks dressing room.

That Game 7 versus the Houston Rockets seems like ages ago. It's always great to run into John at The Garden now and then, and he's still one of the most popular Knicks of all time. It will be fitting if perhaps he can get a job in the Knicks organization. He has done so much for the team and the city. The reason I feel New Yorkers loved John so much was because he was authentic, bold, driven, gave 200 percent, and crazy—that was John Starks on the court.

–Spike Lee
Filmmaker
Brooklyn, New York
July 19, 2004

ACKNOWLEDGMENTS

I would like to thank Dan Markowitz for putting together an inspiring book. Thanks to my uncle, Curtis West, for being there for me, as well as my cousins and the rest of my entire family.

I'd like to thank Greg Anthony, Patrick Ewing, Herb Williams, Jeff Van Gundy, and Allan Houston for being a part of this book. Special thanks to Coach Pat Riley for believing in me when others did not. Thanks to all my coaches who helped me along the way.

To my brother Monty, who helped me during that crucial time in my life—thank you. I'd like to thank Spike Lee for all of your help with this book, but more importantly for being a friend. May God continue to bless you.

If I missed anyone, forgive me. Thanks once again and God Bless.

–John Starks

Foremost, I'd like to thank John Starks for opening up to me about his life, both the struggles and the triumphs. I asked John countless questions and he never dodged a one. Thanks to John's brothers, Vincent ("Monty"), Lawrence (JuJu) and Tony, and to John's wife, Jackie, for their candor. The New York Knicks public relations people, Jonathan Supranowitz and Sammy Steinlight, were very helpful, as well as the team's historian, Dennis D'Agostino. The president of Madison Square Garden, Steve Mills, and Madison Square Garden Network producer, Howie Singer, produced some helpful game tapes. Pat Riley and Greg Anthony filled me in on John Starks's important role on the Knicks teams of the 1990s.

My agent, John Monteleone, played an indispensable role in advising me at the beginning stages of how to write a book through the eyes of an athlete-folk hero and all the people at Sports Publishing L.L.C. have been great. But in particular, I bonded and enjoyed my interaction with my editor, Noah Amstadter, a true basketball fan and wise and friendly man. Thanks to Joey Gironda, an old classmate and basketball team-mate of mine at Rye Neck High School, who met with me for lunch and discussed the project. Gary Lieberman, the Westchester Wildfire owner, was also a boon to the book.

A book like this could never have been written without the culture of basketball in the city of New York and its surrounding areas and the fans who love John Starks, the Knicks and the game. Growing up in New York, having been a Knick fan from the days of Clyde, Reed, DeBusschere, Bradley, Barnett and Cazzie, I have shared a passion with so many other New Yorkers who have flooded the Garden to be lifted by the game's magic. I remember as a kid sitting in the second-to-last row of the Garden's blue seats as the Knicks played the Baltimore Bullets in the 1970 playoffs and feeling an excitement I can never outlive. When a long Bradley or DeBusschere jump shot went in, the crashing applause of the crowd sounded to me like a giant chandelier had fallen onto the court.

That love and excitement fueled me in writing this book.

–Dan Markowitz

INTRODUCTION
FEAST OR FAMINE

"Feast or Famine," Pat Riley's nickname for John Starks

I played 13 years in the National Basketball Association, 866 regular-season games and 96 playoff games and scored 1,352 points in eight playoff series for the New York Knicks, a total topped only by Patrick Ewing, Walt Frazier and Willis Reed in Knicks history. But many people seem to only remember my dunk over Michael Jordan in the 1993 playoffs and how I shot two for 18 in Game 7 of the 1994 Finals. That's sports for you, the ecstasy and the agony. It's what people store in their memory banks.

I'd like to focus mostly on my life before "The Dunk" and my meltdown in Houston, because I think once you read about what I went through before I ever stepped inside an NBA arena, you'll understand who I am a lot better than if I just talk about what happened on those two nights. But for all the fans that still come up to me ten years later and the first things out of their mouths are either: "What made you try to dunk over Horace Grant and Michael Jordan with a playoff game on the line?" or "How come you kept shooting the ball in Game 7?" All right, I'll tell you. But both answers have a history to them.

The first game I ever played for the New York Knicks was back on December 7, 1990, and it was against Michael Jordan and the Chicago Bulls in Chicago. I'd missed the first 16 games of the season with a sprained left knee because of a mid-air collision with Patrick Ewing on the last day of practice before the final team cuts were made. The Knicks were going to cut me, so I tried to do something spectacular by dunking over Patrick on a fast break, but he threw me down like a rag doll, injuring my knee, and I started the year on the injured reserve. But I was healthy and ready to go by the Chicago game, especially because it was against Michael.

I wore No. 32 at Oklahoma State because my favorite player at that time was Magic Johnson, but I had always studied Michael Jordan's game. I used to watch all the Bulls games when I played at Oklahoma State and whenever we were playing on the road, I would have my wife Jackie tape the games so I could watch Michael play when I got back. Chicago was the team I liked, and I liked Michael because he played my position.

The Knicks coach, John McLeod, took Gerald Wilkins out of the game and looked down the bench at me and said, "Let's go, John," and I sprinted onto the court and started guarding Jordan. As soon as I put my hand on his back, he swatted it off and said, "You're going to be calling me Mr. Jordan after the game."

"We'll see," I said.

Now I knew Jordan's game like a book from watching him so much on television. I'd played him like 1,500 times in my mind. Charles Oakley, my new teammate on the Knicks and Jordan's former teammate on the Bulls, told me to play him physical, and McLeod—Stu Jackson had been fired two games earlier—told me to force Michael as much as possible toward the center of the court, toward Patrick.

But watching Michael Jordan on television all those times didn't prepare me for his will. Michael's will was tremendous, and I sensed it as soon as I stood next to him on the court that night. Just because of who he was, he willed his teammates to play above their heads and sent fear into his opponents. Just looking into his eyes, I could tell how hungry and determined he was.

But I'd learned about playing hard from playing in the parks in Tulsa against guys much older than me. I'd played against Dennis Rodman, Karl Malone and Moses Malone in the Pig's

Pop-Off, a big summer league tournament held in Tulsa, before I even made a name for myself back in Oklahoma playing junior college ball. I learned how to play with reckless abandon. If it's in you, it's in you. You're going to go out there and compete. Everyone can play hard, but competing is a different matter. It's the player who can bring that fire and excitement out, who has the toughness to compete in any game.

I knew I couldn't stop Michael—no one stopped Michael Jordan—but I made him work hard for everything he got that night. For the ten minutes I was in the game, I made it real hard on him. I wasn't nervous, because I knew I belonged in the NBA and was out to prove it. I was excited to show what I could do. I've never played with any fear. Fear is for losers. You've got to compete every time you step on the floor.

I never was afraid of guarding anyone. I kept telling myself, over and over again, "Michael Jordan is human." My attitude toward him was the same as it was for everyone else I guarded. I stepped into his face and held my ground. I wasn't going to back down and give in to him just because he was Michael Jordan. I figured Michael and the other players in the NBA should be afraid of me, very afraid. They didn't know me. They didn't know what I could do!

I only scored four points against Michael in that first game, but the following year in a regular-season game at Madison Square Garden against the Bulls, I scored 28 points and then in Game 6 of the Eastern Conference Semifinals I scored my then-career-playoff-high 27 points and held Michael to 21 points. In 1992-93, we beat the Bulls in three out of four regular-season contests, including the season finale where I scored 22 points, hitting on eight of 13 field goals. Michael scored 21 points and took 26 shots. He shot only 35.4 percent from the field during the four games.

So we were feeling confident when we met the Bulls in the Eastern Conference Finals in 1993. They were the two-time NBA defending champions and had beaten us in seven hard-fought games in the Eastern Conference Semifinals in 1992, but we had just knocked off the Indiana Pacers and Charlotte Hornets decisively in the first two rounds of the playoffs. We also had the home-court advantage after winning 60 games in the regular season while Chicago won only 57.

We won Game 1 of the series, 98-90, at the Garden. In the first four minutes and 30 seconds of the fourth quarter, I hit four three-pointers and finished with 25 points. Michael scored 27 points, but connected on only ten of 27 shots and three of 13 in the second half.

After the game, I grabbed a bite to eat with Jackie and then went right back home to Stamford, Connecticut, and watched a replay of the game, something I did after every home game, regular season and playoffs, to see where I could improve for the next game. I read in the papers the next day—this is before I stopped reading the New York papers altogether—that Jordan said:

"Starks played extremely well defensively. He really bodied me up physically and he got me in tough situations where I didn't really get the shot I wanted. I had a tough shooting night, and you have to credit him because he was the guy guarding me. He's as much a surprise to me as he is to you guys. I don't remember when he was in the CBA. I don't remember when he came into the league. But I know he's here now."

I was feeling good, really good. I felt like I was starring on Broadway in The King and I. The year before Jordan had called me "cocky," but now he was saying, "Starks's cockiness has turned into confidence."

But Michael was wrong. I was still cocky. I've always played that way. Off the court I was like Dr. Jekyl, laidback, but on the court, I was Mr. Hyde, a totally different person. When I took the court, I had to leave it all out there and basically destroy the person who was guarding me. I'd rather be a cocky player than a player who doesn't believe in his ability.

I knew I could play with anyone. I didn't come into the NBA with all the bells and whistles of being a high draft choice. I had to go back down to the CBA before I ever made a name for myself in the league. That's why a lot of people didn't give me a chance to make it. But I came in and beat out some players by pure determination and heart.

Game 1 had been on a Sunday, and Game 2, on May 25, 1993, was a Tuesday night. The Garden was rocking even before the warmups began. The fans were putting out a lot of energy. They wanted to beat the Bulls as much as we did. We hated the Bulls because of the preferential treatment they got from the refs and how they still always bellyached about calls, especially Phil Jackson. He was always saying ridiculous things like calling our physical style of play "basketbrawling." But mostly, we hated them because they had what we wanted: championships.

I had a pretty quiet game offensively, scoring only 12 points on 11 shots, but all my points came in the second half, and I was playing aggressive defense on Michael. He took 32 shots and only made 12, scoring 25 points. With one minute remaining in the game, we were up by three, 91-88, but the Bulls were closing, just having gone on an 8-3 run.

I had the ball on the left baseline with the shot clock winding down. I'd noticed throughout the game that B. J. Armstrong, my defender, had been overplaying me up top, trying to deny me from running the pick and roll with Patrick, our favorite play. I knew that when I wanted to, one time, I'd have the opening to go along the baseline to get to the basket.

Patrick must've been thinking the same thing, because when he came out to set the pick, drawing Bulls center Bill Cartwright away from the basket, instead of setting it up top like usual, he came inside of Armstrong and picked him off. I saw the opening and stormed along the baseline to the basket as Horace Grant sprinted out to meet me. I knew I had to go strong because he's long at six foot ten.

I hit the baseline so quick, I took two dribbles and I was up in the air. If you jump early, you can catch a lot of big guys while they're still running out on you because they're often late in getting over. When I jumped I didn't realize I was so far out from the basket. All I saw was Grant and the basket and I just kept rising. I didn't see Jordan at all and I wasn't looking for him.

To tell you the truth, I didn't see Jordan until I saw the picture of "The Dunk" in the paper the next day, his mouth wide open—but with no tongue wagging—his left hand reaching net high while mine was up over the rim. Michael came too late, but the way I went in with my left hand, it wouldn't have mattered if he were in the paint waiting for me. I still would've dunked it.

Once you dunk over your first big man, there's no going back. I didn't start dunking on a regulation, 10-foot basket until I was 18 years old, so dunking was always exciting to me. I'd dunked against seven-footers before, like Sam Bowie and Hakeem Olajuwon, going in with my left hand, so I knew I could go in hard over anybody and throw it down. Dunking with my left hand while I drove to the basket going right was my signature dunk. When I was still an unknown on the Tulsa playgrounds, I made a name for myself by dunking over Anthony Bowie, who was a big-time player then for the University of Oklahoma, by switching the ball from my right to left hand in mid-air and throwing it down with authority.

I'm not going to lie to you, dunking the ball that way in a game that big in front of that Garden crowd felt good. It felt as good as anything can feel in this world. But it didn't all register with me until much later, far after the dunk and the game. When I dunked the ball, I knew I had to run hard down court to get back on defense. I knew the Bulls were going to come right back down at us. They always pushed the ball hard after a made basket to try to get something quick.

Mostly, it's been people mentioning "The Dunk" to me—probably a million times—that has made me realize how big a play it was, especially for Knicks fans. They tell me, "Hey, that was the greatest dunk ever, that move you made against the Bulls in the '93 playoffs." It makes me feel great that people remember me for something that made them feel so good. Because then there are those other people who think when they see me that my name is: "Game 7, Houston, two for 18, what happened?"

I don't have a simple answer. I know what type of a player I was, and I know that I was a much better player than what I showed in that one game. Some guys have the chance to make up for playing badly in a championship game by playing great in another championship game, but I never got that second chance. Dennis Johnson shot zero for 14 and scored four points in the seventh game of the 1978 Finals, and his team, the Seattle SuperSonics, lost, but the following year they won the championship, and then he won two more championships with the Boston Celtics. I shot three for 18 in the first game of the '94 Finals and scored only 11 points, but I recovered in the next five games of the series to score 105 points on 34-of-70 shooting from the field.

I was capable of playing a lot better. I had played a lot better in the four games preceding Game 7, scoring in double digits in the fourth quarter of each game. I dreamed about being in games like that against Houston, 48 minutes to win a championship. I loved pressure games and taking the big shots at the end.

My motto as a shooter was: "If I miss one, the next one has to fall." If you're a shooter, if you have confidence in your shot, you've got to keep shooting. I firmly believed that if I missed five in a row, I'd make the next ten in a row. That turned out to be wrong in Game 7, but that's what I believed, and guys who don't shouldn't be out on the court at the end of a big game.

Patrick and Oak sometimes got upset with me for shooting too much, but I knew deep down inside, they didn't mind seeing the ball in my hands at the end of a game. Because they knew I wanted it. No matter what had happened up to that point, when the game was on the line, I wanted to take the big shot. That's why I think Pat Riley kept me in Game 7, even as I missed all ten of the shots I took in the fourth quarter.

People have selective memories. They forget that in Game 6 I scored 16 points in the fourth quarter, and if Olajuwon hadn't tipped my last shot, a three from the left corner with two seconds left, we would've won the championship. It's as simple as that. When that ball left my hand, I knew it was going in. Hakeem, why couldn't you have let me have it?

I felt like I had to repeat Game 6, the way I played in the fourth quarter, in Game 7, and I put too much pressure on myself. I felt like I had to have an even bigger game in Game 7, and I let my emotions get the best of me. I didn't sleep at all the night before the game. I probably needed an outlet, someone to talk to, but I'm the kind of person who keeps to himself when preparing for a big game.

I probably had too much time to think about it, because there were two days off between Game 6 and Game 7, and for most of the time I sat up in that hotel room in Houston going over in my head every step of Game 6. I've wished many times since that we were at home during that time and I had my family around to distract me or the team had moved to a different location so we could've gotten out of Houston.

I couldn't believe Hakeem had gotten his fingertips on my shot. I was sure that I had cleared him and between replaying Game 6 and thinking of Game 7, it's almost all I thought of, and that ended up hurting me. I felt like I had to be the one to get us over the hump.

I cried after the game. I was heartbroken. We had worked so hard to get there—playing 25 playoff games, still an NBA record—and for me to go out and have a game like that was horrible. I took every loss hard, but if I could erase that one game and win a championship for the Knick fans, I'd do it in a second. Knicks fans deserve a championship, and as a player I wanted to win one for the city more than anything. It just didn't work out.

A lot of people thought that after Game 7 my career would go down the tubes; I'd be devastated. I wouldn't be able to perform again under the pressure. But I played four more seasons in New York and won the Sixth Man of the Year award in 1996 when Allan Houston took over as the starting shooting guard.

Game 7 took a lot out of me. Fans and reporters—for months afterward—wanted to talk to me about it. That stuff wore me down. I stopped reading the papers. I didn't want to think about that game, and I didn't watch the tape of it until the middle of the following season, and only then to finally exorcise it from my mind.

A lot of people thought, even Coach Riley, that I'd lost some of the respect of my teammates because of Game 7, but I didn't feel that they treated me any differently. Sure, I heard some of them call me "Riley's son" a bit more, but some of them also told me that they knew they wouldn't have gotten to a Game 7 in the Finals if it weren't for me. Everyone has bad games. It was just unfortunate that I had a bad game in the biggest game of my life.

It was hard, but it was still a game and nothing as tough as what I'd survived growing up. All I've ever known is working hard and surviving. Where I came from, what I went through and saw my brothers, my mother, my grandmother and my friends go through, I was lucky to be alive to play in Game 7. I'd been through too much to let one game get me down.

I've had a lot of low points in my life, and I knew how to come back from desperate situations. I wasn't going to forget where I came from or the path I took from playing on the hard-top in Cheyenne Park in North Tulsa to playing in the Mecca of basketball, Madison Square Garden. We're all park players in the NBA, or at least we once all were, and it's a park type of a game out there. North Tulsa is a long way from New York City, but I still feel now the hunger I felt as a kid and how I struggled back then.

CHAPTER 1

DON'T TAKE NOTHING FROM NOBODY

"His whole career, John has been told, 'No, you can't do it.' It developed his unique temperament: one of innocence combined with a defiant, combative competitiveness."

—Pat Riley, John Starks's coach with the New York Knicks

I was born on August 10, 1965, in Tulsa, Oklahoma, and except for two years when I was five and my mother moved the family out to Los Angeles, I stayed in or around Tulsa until I was 23. I was the third of five brothers—Tony, Vincent, me, Lynn and Lawrence—and then there were my two sisters, Anita and Nicole. Except for Lawrence and Anita, we all had different fathers. My mother, Irene Starks, and my grandmother, Callie West, looked after us all, but my grandmother had her own place, separate from ours.

My family lived pretty much all over North Tulsa. North Tulsa is where all the black folks lived. It was nice. It wasn't run down, although there were spots worse than others. We lived in houses and apartment complexes, and only once for a short time did we live in the deep North section of Tulsa, where the neighborhoods were a lot rougher and most of the drugs were dealt. Tulsa is a friendly city, but it can be dangerous, too. My brother Vincent, who we called "Monty," said that one year in the 1980s, Tulsa was statistically second to only Washington D.C. in murders nationwide and first in car thefts. The deep North is where most of those murders and car thefts occurred.

My family moved into our first house on Virgin Street when I was born. Before us, the previous owners of the house had been a white family. Talking to my mother and my two older brothers, moving into the house on Virgin Street felt like moving into a whole new world. We had never lived in a neighborhood with white folks before. I lived in the house on Virgin Street, off and on, until I was eight years old, and as more black folks started moving into the neighborhood, most of the white folks left and moved up into the bigger houses up on Reservoir Hill.

We used to wander up Reservoir Hill all the time and look at the houses and say, "One day, we're going to get up here." That was our dream as little kids. Reservoir Hill overlooks the city and many of the houses have beautiful views. I thought of moving a lot when I was a kid, because it was a normal occurrence for me. We moved 11 or 12 times as I was growing up, sometimes in the middle of the night because we didn't have the rent money.

My mother always scouted out places for us to live. We lived in the Morningstar apartments just after they were built, before all the trouble started years after we left there. Monty and Lawrence—my youngest brother, who we called Ju Ju—later sold cocaine inside that complex. But when we first moved in, it had a nice, big swimming pool and a little store that few people on the outside knew about, because it was run illegally. It was a nice setup.

During my grade school years, mostly we lived in two-bedroom houses with a den and a kitchen. In the house on Virgin Street, there were 16 of us—two families, my four brothers and two sisters and me, my mother, my four cousins, my uncles Curtis and Lawrence and my aunt Betty, and my grandmother—all sleeping in two rooms. The 12 kids all slept in bunk beds stacked on top of each other all the way up to the ceiling. We had to slide into bed like sardines.

It was two kids to a bed, and I didn't want to sleep with the younger kids because when one of them peed in the sheets, I'd wake up with it all over me. All the kids would sneak back into the kitchen after the adults were asleep and make crazy sandwiches like peanut butter and bologna. If my grandmother caught us, she'd grab her belt and whip our butts. We weren't supposed to eat after dinner, but we never got enough to eat. In the morning, I'd wake up with a killer bellyache.

We all had nicknames. Vince was "Monty," I was "Johnty," Lynn was "Bucky," Lawrence was "Ju Ju," Tony was "T," Anita was "Pooky" and Nicole was "Nikki." Tony and Monty played football on their high school team—Tony was the starting cornerback—Monty the starting free safety, and I always tried to do what they did. I was four years younger than Tony and three years younger than Monty, so they roughed me up a lot.

My grandmother would kick us out of the house in the summer and tell us she didn't want to see any of us until five o'clock. There were all kinds of sports to play and competition all the time. All I did growing up was compete against my brothers and friends. Even in the house we played football and clothes-hanger basketball, where we used to hang a clothes hanger on the top of a door and shoot a rolled-up sock through it. We didn't have a basketball goal so we created one indoors. We'd bang up against the walls and my grandmother would come into our room and say, "What is it y'all are doing in here?"

Sometimes my grandmother would come outside and play with us. She was only about five foot tall, but she used to come out into the yard and throw us passes. My grandmother made us go from football to basketball to baseball. My mother didn't much care for sports, but my grandmother was a sports addict. I even played a little tennis, because my Uncle Curtis was an All-American tennis player at Northeastern State University in Tahlequah, Oklahoma. Inspired by Arthur Ashe, a lot of young black kids played tennis when he grew up in the 1960s and 1970s.

Monty was an All-American football player at Nathan Hale High School in Tulsa. His father was Johnny Lewis, who played four seasons of major league baseball. In 1965, Johnny Lewis was the best hitter on the New York Mets, batting .245 and smacking 15 home runs. He later was the third base coach for the St. Louis Cardinals. When Monty was around 12, the Cardinals played against their AAA minor league team in Tulsa, the Tulsa Drillers, and Monty went and got Bob Gibson's and Lou Brock's autographs. His dad told Monty to write him and he did, but Monty never heard back from Johnny Lewis.

Monty was the best all-around athlete in the family. By the time he was 13, he was built and looked a lot like Lawrence Taylor and was just as tough. I never played against anyone in the NBA as tough as Monty. All four of my brothers and I, along with the other neighborhood kids, would play football in the street. I played wide receiver in the park leagues until my mother steered me away from football. She thought I wasn't big enough, and it was too aggressive a game and I might get hurt.

The best catch and hit I ever saw was when Monty led Bucky with a pass that made him crash right into a parked car. Right when Bucky caught the ball, he slammed into the car, knocking him down, but he held onto the ball. It was the last time Bucky ever played football with us. But it was an amazing play.

You had to be tough in our family. If someone called one of us a "punk" or a "sissy," those were fighting words. There was nothing soft about any one of us. Monty likes to say that he taught me desire and the attitude of: "Don't take no kind of mess from nobody." If I got into a fight and lost, Monty would find out about it and make me go back and fight the kid again, but this time in front of him—and I had to win. He'd tell me, "You don't lose fights in our family."

Fighting was something all my brothers and sisters and I were very familiar with growing up. The first rule in our family was to mind our mother and grandmother, Callie West, and the second was not to back down from a fight. Tony and Monty fought each other almost on a daily basis. It was big brother against little brother, even though they were only a year apart in age. Tony was trying to keep control of the household while Monty was trying to gain control. My younger brothers and sisters and I would sit back and watch them fight.

We got our fighting spirits from both my mother and my grandmother. They were small women in stature, but they didn't back down from anyone. I remember once when I was eight years old, the toilet backed up on me while we were living in my Auntie Iona Grayson's house on Xyler Street. She moved to California, so we moved into her house. The plumbing was messed up, so when I flushed the toilet my stool backed up into the tub.

My grandmother walked in and said, "What in the world have you done, you nasty rat? You're going to have to bail that out."

"I'm not bailing that out," I said.

"Get your butt down there," she said "and bail that stuff out."

Like I said, you didn't cross my grandmother. I got down on the floor and started bailing the tub out and I had tears running down my face, it was so bad. My brothers came by the door laughing and making fun of me. But Tony went too far. He got my grandmother so angry that she took off her shoe, and as he ran away from her down the hall, she threw it and nailed him with it in the back of his head.

My mother had a lot of trouble with the men in her life. She was very unlucky with the men she chose. She was a very beautiful woman, short with cocoa skin, and she really knew how to dress. She was married three times, but never to my father. I was in college the last time my mother got married. When she wasn't married, she would date occasionally and, depending on what these men could bring to the table, some of the men she dated would move in with us.

Looking back on it now, as I do a great deal—sometimes I wish I wouldn't, but I can't help it, I'm a thinker by nature—I believe my mother was looking for a father figure. Like my brothers and sisters and I, except for Tony—she didn't have her father on a daily basis. When my grandmother moved back to Tulsa from Los Angeles, my mother's father, Harold Starks, stayed out in Los Angeles. My mother only saw him during the summers. That's why I think she was always looking for a man to take care of her. All these cats out on the streets sensed that, and they'd say to my mother, "I'll take care of you."

My mother got into terrible fistfights with some of the men in her life. I was just a kid, and I didn't like seeing anyone messing with my mother. But she was a real tough lady, a fighter. She never backed down from anyone.

It was disturbing to watch these men beat up on her and see her bleed and hit them back. Despite being only five foot four, she was a woman who could handle herself in a fight.

My mother was scared of guns, but the men who stayed with us kept guns in the house that she would get her hands on. She used one of those guns to shoot and almost kill Nikki's daddy. These were knock-down, drag-out fights with blood and bruises, and it created a strong, ugly tension in the household.

One time in the middle of a fight, my mother ran out of the house and got into her car to get away from this man. He chased her, and as she was pulling out, he grabbed onto the car door handle and she drove halfway down the street with him still hanging onto the car door handle. I don't know what he was thinking trying to stop a moving car. It was like something you see in a movie, it was just crazy.

I never knew when I lay down to sleep at one or two o'clock in the morning when a fight might start. The police showed up sometimes at the different houses we lived in, and it was embarrassing to see police cars out in front of your house and everyone in the neighborhood outside their houses watching. That probably explains why I'm a light sleeper today.

Whenever my mother got into fights, I would call my grandmother and tell her, "She's up here fighting." Tony and Monty were living with my grandmother by then, and she'd always send Monty or Tony up to stop the fights. My uncles sometimes would try to stop the fights, but they weren't always around. Lawrence was mostly out on the streets, and Curtis was away at college.

Monty, at 10 or 11 years old, stood up to these men. I can remember one time waiting for Monty to show up, and when he didn't come right away I picked up this kitchen knife and had crazy thoughts on my mind. I wanted to kill the man who was battering my mother. But then Monty came through the door.

These men didn't care about the kids in our family who were not their own. They didn't feel committed to us. Our house was just a place to lay their heads. Lawrence and Anita's dad, Buster Peoples, lived with us the longest. My mother and he lived together for about five years until he died in a car crash. This was back in the 1970s, and Buster was a drummer in a band. Drugs were everywhere. Everybody was doing everything, and I'm pretty sure Buster was doing a lot of stuff. When his band went out to Los Angeles for a while when I was five, my mother moved the whole family out there with them.

Buster had a lot of anger in him. I'm not sure if he was abused as a child, but he beat us kids with a clothes hanger wrapped in thick rope. He treated Lawrence and Anita different than the rest of us. He resented the fact that we weren't his kids. He hated that my mother had other children besides his own. He used to try to make us eat menthol, but I used to outsmart him by sitting with my back to the window and when he wasn't looking, I would dump all the menthol out the window and then pretend that I ate it.

We all got in the middle of my mother's fights with Buster and the rest of these men. We'd yell at my mother and the men, "Stop it! Stop it!" We'd tell my mother to leave, but there was nowhere to go. These men lived with us. My mother was under a lot of stress to provide for us, and she did the best she could. She used to tell us all the time, "You have to get through it. Just deal with it."

She was a young mother with seven kids to bring up. She didn't have time to do much of anything but survive. My mother worked as a nurse, she worked in a beauty salon, and for a while, she owned a laundromat. She taught me how to drive when I was 13 years old, and I used to drive her car—it was a little bitty thing called a Champ—from our house on Denver Street to the laundromat.

But my mother worked all kinds of odd jobs as well, and when her jobs stressed her out, we would get back on welfare or another man would appear in our lives. It wasn't like we were the only family in North Tulsa going through hard times. I had friends whose mothers had the same problems. We just had to get through it.

My mother was a tough woman. She enjoyed going out on the weekends and having fun. She was a free spirit, but cautious, too. She enjoyed people and I got my people skills from her. It made me feel good to see my mother enjoy herself when she had so many tough times. I think back to those times and I wonder what our lives could have been like if we had a place to call our own. I love my mother very much and I know in my heart that she tried to take care of us the best way that she knew how. Even so, those fights affected all of my brothers and sisters growing up.

I think my combativeness on the basketball court goes back to those days when I watched my mother get beat by so many men. Watching her go through what she did built a lot of anger in me. But seeing her display so much heart through all of her ups and downs, trials and tribulations, I learned her survival skills. All of what my mother went through and how she handled became a part of me.

As I got a little older, I would block out of my mind the violence I saw my mother go through by taking my ball and going down to the court in Cheyenne Park or at Burroughs Elementary School and spend hours shooting baskets. Basketball was my salvation. For as long as I can remember, playing basketball always made me feel better. A basketball court was always the place where I could shut my mind off and just play.

Monty was older and right in the middle of all the fighting that went on, so he remembers more of it than I do.

Monty Lewis:

It'd be two or three o'clock in the morning, and my mother would be fighting with Billy, her boyfriend. I was in the fourth or fifth grade and John would call my grandmother's house and tell her they were fighting again. My grandmother would wake me up and say, "Monty, go up there and see about your Mama."

I'd have to walk two or three miles sometimes. My grandmother's house was on Virgin Street, and my mother and the rest of the family would stay in different places. I was in the fourth grade walking up and down the damn streets at three or four in the morning going to see what was going on. I'd get to the house and go inside, and there'd be blood all over the house, you'd think your Mama was dead. That's just how it was. Walking up there, you didn't know what you were likely to see.

I remember when I was younger, and Buster was staying with us up in a house on Emerson Street and he was beating up on her for a whole day. We had to stay in our room. So I picked up all the kids and put them out the window, and we walked all the way down to my grandmother's house in the middle of the night. I was around ten and John was seven. It was all up to me to make sure that everyone was all right.

Grandma told me I had to take care of all the other kids in the family. She sat me down and said, "Monty, you and Tony are the oldest, and you're the biggest. You've got to look after the kids." What Granny said was the Bible. I did what she told me.

Buster used to whip us all night when we were real young and living in south central Los Angeles, on Second Street and Washington Avenue. It got to the point where I used to dream of killing him, and I would've if he was still around when I got to an age where I was big enough, no more than 13, to do it. I used to dream all the time of getting strong enough to kill him.

He'd put menthol in our mouths and tell us to eat it. He did all kinds of cruel stuff to all of the kids in the family. When we were out in Los Angeles we were isolated, far away from grandma, so we had no one to turn to for help. If we did something wrong, our mother would whip us, but she didn't come after us for no reason like Lawrence's dad did.

I hated him so much that to this day, if he was still alive, I'd try to kill him. When we moved back to Tulsa, it finally got to the point where my grandmother said to my mother, "Are you going to stay with him or take care of your kids? Because he can't come around here no more."

Being just a kid and listening to a man beat your mother and hearing your mother scream, we used to hurt a lot. Every time we heard a loud noise or heard something hit the wall, we'd think imme-diately, "Mama's in a fight again." It just happened so often.

When the family was by ourselves, we'd do fairly decent. But the moment my mother brought home a boyfriend, it'd bring us down. We'd have no food, no money to pay the bills, and we'd have to move out of houses in the middle of the night.

We told my mother all our lives—my grandmother did too, and our neighbors—not to get involved with these men. But my mother was the kind of person who didn't give a damn what other people thought. She'd get with these men who were half-assed pimps who'd been in and out of penitentiaries, were ex-drug addicts, but she'd stick with them and stick with them. When they got into fights, she'd pull out knives and go at them. She almost killed my little sister, Nicole's, daddy.

I remember one day when we were all small kids my mother came out of the bathroom and gave us all a hug and said, "Mommy might not ever see you all again." Later that night I was watching the news on television, and I saw her and my Uncle Lawrence. They had shot Nicole's daddy down on North Peoria Street. He had tried to make my mother shoot water in her veins and she wouldn't go for it. It makes your body feel like it's burning up. He was angry with her because she wouldn't go out on the street to make money.

The next day she shot him six times and reloaded and shot him two more times but still didn't kill him. She pleaded self-defense and told the police that he had beaten her that day when actually it'd been the day before. The police had been called up to the house so many times that there was a history of their fights, and she got off.

My mother was a hustler. She did what she had to do in order for us to survive. She was a survivor. Whatever guy she was with, if he stopped making money and brought nothing home to help out the family, she'd tell him he'd have to go if he didn't start doing some-thing. I beat up her boyfriends and threw them out of the house when I got old enough.

She never apologized to us about what happened. She'd say, "Deal with it." And if things got too crazy, she'd tell us to go down and stay at our grandmother's house. Granny wasn't too happy about that. She'd raised her four kids on her own pretty much. She got tired of us, but she never turned us away. She tried to make us do the right thing, but if we did wrong, she was always there to help us out.

When I got old enough, 13 or 14, I moved out of both my mother's and grandmother's houses and stayed at my girlfriend's house. I started selling drugs in the far north and I was making a lot of money. I got the drugs from family members out in Los Angeles. They would send it back to me or I would go out and get it. I was the first person to bring rock cocaine to Tulsa back in 1981. I would pay $300 for an ounce and make $3,200. It was booming back then.

I made enough money that at one point I had three houses. I gave one to my mother, because she and her boyfriend had gotten into a fight and she and the kids didn't have anywhere else to go. I started buying food for the family. I was tired of seeing them move from place to place. It's fortunate that I had a street sense. I had been on the streets all my life. I woke up on the streets.

Monty and I dealt with the tension in our family differently. Monty would fume when my mother and Buster would eat steak while the rest of us ate stew. But as long as I was eating, I was happy. My mother wouldn't eat all her steak anyway, and then she'd let us go get the steak.

CHAPTER 2

GIMME THE ROCK

"John's the type of person where it kills him not to play basket-ball."

—Charles Smith, teammate of John Starks

I was seven years old when I first picked up a basketball in my neighbor's backyard. There was a piece of plywood nailed into a pole for the backboard and a bicycle tire rim attached to the backboard no more than eight feet off the ground. The yard was grass except for a patch of dirt around the basket.

One time, my cousin Antonio and I laid a trashcan on its side in front of the basket and I ran and jumped off of it. I was up in the air, floating, and then I dunked the ball. That is what really got me hooked. I'd seen Dr. J on television dunking, and I decided right then that I was going to play in the NBA one day just like Dr. J.

I was a short and scrawny kid—at 18 years old I was still only five foot ten—but I loved basketball from that first day I picked up a ball. I immediately liked the way it felt in my hands when I rolled it back and forth. As I got older, I started going down to Cheyenne Park after school and playing in the pickup games. I'd take the bus home and do my homework, or a lot of times just skip my homework (the only subject I liked was math), and I'd go down to the park with my ball. Even in Tulsa, when 100-degree summer days are the norm, I played basketball in the parks for hours.

I always shined on the playground. You had to earn your stripes down at the park. Everyone had the Dr. J finger roll and wanted to dunk like the Doctor. I had a big afro like Dr. J, too. I cut my teeth down in the parks playing ball, and I made a name for myself. I played decent defense, had a good shot, could dribble the ball, and I always had confidence in my game.

When I go back now to the area where I grew up, I don't see as many young players in the parks like when I was younger. You could find good basketball everywhere in North Tulsa back then. I played in Cheyenne Park, Chamberlain, BC Franklin, Ben Hill and Owen Park. They were all about a 10- to 15-minute bike ride from one another, and I had my homemade bike made from different parts that I'd jump on and go find games. In some parks, there'd be 40 to 50 guys waiting on the sidelines to play. So if you lost, you were down five or six games and you just had to wait your turn or go to another park.

Growing up in North Tulsa, you had to be good at some kind of sport to get respect. It was the best way to impress the girls. And even though I was just a scrawny kid, I thought I could play against anybody. I'd pick the best player on the opposing team and always check him.

I used to play one on one against a good friend of mine named Richard Thompson. I saw him as the wall I had to climb to become a really good player. Richard was on the high school team. We used to play one on one until it got dark and then play until the streetlights went out. We'd play one on one until midnight. We didn't stop until we were too tired from beating up on each other.

I was fiercely competitive from battling my brothers and always trying to beat them. It was instilled in me from an early age, and it helped me not back down against bigger, older kids in the park. If Richard couldn't make it down to the park, I'd shoot alone, making up games in which I competed against myself, shooting jumper after jumper.

My grandmother would tell Tony and Monty that they had to take me with them when they left the house to play sports, and she'd tell me that I had to keep up. That's why even as a little kid I always thought that I was older than I was. My brothers and I had a contest to see who could get the most trophies up on my grandmother's living room mantle. It was the first thing you saw when you walked into her house, all our trophies lined up on her mantle.

• • •

My father's name was Ray McGee. For a while after I was born, he worked construction and lived in Tulsa. I knew where he lived. My mother and I visited him a couple of times, but when he left Tulsa when I was around three years old, I never remember my mother ever talking about him again. All I can remember about him is that he was tall. When he moved away from Tulsa, I never saw him again.

Tony's father was around and stayed involved in his life, but Monty only saw his father that one time at the ball field. That's the way so many black men behaved back then. They just did their thing and left. A guy would go off for a job and never come back. Very few cared about the kids they left behind.

Tony didn't get into as much trouble as the rest of us, because his father was around and would come by and pick him up and they'd go off and do things together. Monty and I didn't have that, and I think we both would've benefited from having fathers in our lives. I'd look at other kids at school who had both parents in their household and I'd see their fathers attend their games, but my father never came. At school functions I'd feel embarrassed and angry at times that I didn't have a father who would show up and care about me. My mother would show up sometimes, and when she couldn't come, my grandmother would fill in. But I remember wanting a father as a kid, and it hurt me not to have one.

Monty had all the ability to play in the NFL. Out of high school, a lot of schools recruited him, but he didn't have the grades. He went one year to Northeastern State University in Tahlequah, an NAIA school, and played for a national championship. Oklahoma University wanted him to attend a junior college to get his grades up and then transfer there to play football, but the call of the streets was too strong, and he couldn't let go of the partying.

Monty was forced into a man's role early and hung out with an older crowd. He was smoking weed and drinking by the time he was 12 or 13 years old. He was always fighting and getting kicked out of school. He and I used to get into scrapes, but he was much bigger than me, so I'd just take a couple of blows and that would be it. But I still gravitated toward Monty because he was big on the athletic stage and he was a fighter.

I was pretty much a fun-loving and carefree kid who had a lot of friends in the neighborhood. My cousin, Antonio, was my best friend. He and I lived in the same house for many years growing up. We were rambunctious kids. We got ourselves in a lot trouble, but nothing serious. We used to watch *The Little Rascals* a lot, and we acted like them. When we lived on Virgin Street, we built this tree house for ourselves. We used to bring our sleeping bags up into it and stay all night. We'd play "I Spy" and look down at kids on neighboring blocks and yell out, "Virgin's the best street."

When we lived on Elwood Street, we had these woods behind our backyard, and some of the kids on our block and Antonio and I would go back in there and do crazy things. You'd be amazed what you could find back in those woods. We'd hunt tarantulas and then pit them against each other in fights. We did the same thing with crawdads, find the biggest ones and then have them fight. That was our entertainment. We didn't have video games.

We didn't go on vacations growing up, but every summer we'd go down to Bell's Park in Tulsa—it was like our Disneyland—when the fair came around. I didn't like going on the rides. I used to get a sick feeling in my stomach when I went on one.

Osage Road ran back behind the woods, and we'd go back there and put trash on the road and then go back into the woods. When a driver stopped, we would throw rocks at his car while he was in it and then we'd take off running. A lot of the men would get out of their cars and chase us, but we knew the woods so well, they'd get halfway in and stop. People started hating traveling down Osage Road. Once they saw the trash piled up, they'd stop their cars, do a quick U-turn and go back the way they came.

There were a couple of working oil pumps in our neighborhood. You had to walk through the woods and across Osage Road and they were in a field over in Osage County on an Indian reservation. We used to play on them. They moved up and down like a rocking horse, and we would time it just right, and jump on the back of them and ride them up and down like a see saw. It was dangerous but a lot of fun.

One day, Lawrence tore his foot up in one of them. Instead of jumping up onto the pedestal, he got his foot caught in the pump and it crushed his foot. The doctor thought he was going to have to amputate the foot, but in the end he didn't. Lawrence wound up severely crippled. While he was in the hospital, the doctors gave him morphine for the pain and he became addicted to it. Then he turned to cocaine and developed a very bad habit.

I was too involved with sports to get seriously involved with drinking or drugs when I was still in elementary school and middle school. I was always going to basketball and baseball practices and games. One night after practice, my friends and I decided to ride our skateboards home. My friends and I used to fly down big hills in the pitch dark. We didn't have the nice big, wide skateboards kids have now. We had little, skinny ones. If we hit a rock coming down a hill, the board would jack-knife up into the air and we'd crash. I always thought I could go down any hill, no matter how big it was. We went down this steep hill and could not see the road because it was so dark. When I got down to the bottom of it, I looked back and one of my friends was lying flat out on the road. He hit nothing but pavement.

Whatever I did growing up, I gave my full attention to it. When I was little I used to watch TV, and I would focus in on the television set so intently, especially if it was a show that I was really interested in. My mother would scream and holler for me, but when my mind was set on that TV, I wouldn't hear her. She would come up to me and hit me and say, "Did you hear me? Are you deaf or something?" It was the same way when I played basketball. I didn't hear the fans boo, so it never bothered me. I was always too focused in on the game. That's just how I am.

My family went to the Greater Union Baptist Church. I used to hate to get out of bed and go to Sunday school. My mother used to have to pull us out of our bunk beds. We always wore our shorts underneath our dress slacks for church and long, thick black dress socks over our white tube socks. As soon as we got home from church, we would change and run down to the park and start playing.

But I always felt so much better after I went to church and heard the gospel singing, especially as I got older and started to understand why it made me feel better. Growing up, I saw two different worlds, the everyday, hard world of the streets, and the blessed one in the church. I was reminded every Sunday that I had a choice between living the right way or the wrong way. It came down to making decisions. Going to church, hearing the Word and praying provided a balance in my life.

In the sixth grade, I got caught shoplifting at Safeway, a grocery store chain that I later worked for. I needed a lock for basketball practice and I asked my mother if she could buy it for me, but she said she didn't have the money. So I proceeded to go out and get it myself, and I got caught. When I got home, my mother had already heard about it from the store manager and she laid down the law very, very hard.

We had this oak tree in our backyard and my grandmother made me go out and cut my own switch from the bark of the tree. I couldn't come back with a little switch, because then she'd go out and grab the whole tree. It felt like a death sentence walking out to cut the switch that I knew she was going to use to beat my butt with. It was this mental game not to show my grandmother any fear because then she'd whip me harder. Because of the respect all my brothers had for both my mother and my grandmother, none of us ever stood up to them. Still, sometimes I would run away, and I would hear my mother yelling after me.

"You can try to take off and run, Johnty, but eventually you've got to come back home and it's only going to be worse."

My mother and grandmother were two very strong-willed women and they had to be, because the first five of us were boys. We didn't have the pleasure of having an older sister to look after us. Pooky was a little tomboy and Nikki liked to play with girly things. My mother and grandmother had to be the father as well as the mother, so they had to be tough. For two women, trying to raise five young men was especially difficult. I know personally, once I got to be a certain age, I stopped listening to them, because I felt I'd passed into manhood and that I had to make my own decisions. I felt I had to go out and make my own mistakes.

CHAPTER 3

JOY AND PAIN

"If today wasn't so good, make tomorrow better."

—Irene Starks, John's mother

We lived a humble life. My mother did all she could, but she had seven kids to provide for and boys eat a lot. No matter how tough things ever were for me as a kid, my mother taught me to live day to day. She told me that it was the only way to live. If today was bad, she'd say, get up and make tomorrow better.

We were on welfare—which included food stamps and housing—because my mother was in and out of jobs. Food came into the house at the beginning of the month, and we knew it would last for only two to three weeks before we ate it all up. Then we had to wait until the beginning of the next month for another check to come in. So for about a week or so we were on our own.

We didn't come late to the dinner table, and we hardly got seconds. My mother would say, "You can't be eating all this food," but we were growing boys and we ate a lot. The last week of the month, we used to live on pancakes: breakfast, lunch and dinner, and sometimes only bread and butter and popcorn.

Stealing food was the norm for us. When I was six or seven years old, there was a little grocery store down the street from us called the "Git-n-Go." When we ran out of food, Monty would say to us, "We got to go up to the Git-n-Go and get something to eat."

We had coats on, it was winter. Outside the store, he'd tell me, "I want you to go and get bologna and stuff like that. Meats."

So I'd walk in, and we'd both start stuffing food in our pockets. One time, as we walked out, one of the clerks told us to stop and we just took off. But they knew us—and who our mother was—and when they told her about how we stole food, she came after us. My mother asked Monty and me why we did it and we said, "We're hungry. We did what we had to do."

But she still whupped our butts.

Except it was worth it. I'd have done anything to stop those hunger pains at the end of the month from hitting me. They used to stay with me for a long while, and when I was hungry, my temper spiked quicker. To this day, my wife, Jackie, sees that at times I don't eat. There's plenty of food, but I'll just forget to eat, and then I get frustrated very quickly just like when I was a kid. It's like I don't want to forget how those hunger pains felt.

We grew up with dogs, mostly pit bulls and doberman pinschers. We had a lot of dogs. We liked their toughness. Where we were living, everyone had a tough dog. I couldn't walk down the street with a chihuahua. I wouldn't get any respect. We fed the dogs whatever we ate. If we didn't eat, then they didn't eat.

I didn't take most things to heart as a kid. I never did take anything personally. I just had a very, very forgiving heart, and I still do. My mother was like that, too. If you did something bad to her she might hate you for a while, but she'd eventually forgive you. Basketball also taught me not to take things too personally.

I averaged around 24 points a game in the Mabee Center and Lincoln Park Leagues during fifth and sixth grades, and we won the championship both years. We played a lot of half-court games in the Tulsa playgrounds, and I had developed a deadly outside shot that made me almost unstoppable. But it was at the awards dinner of my sixth-grade year I learned a valuable lesson about individual awards.

My grandmother got all dressed up and came with me to the dinner. I remember thinking that it was important that I receive the Most Valuable Player of the team award. The coach's name was Roy Gage and when he got up to make the announcement, I practically couldn't contain myself, I was so ready to spring out of my seat and accept the MVP trophy.

When Coach Gage said, "The MVP of the team is Bruce Benjamin," I felt sick. Bruce Benjamin was a kid averaging like three points per game! I got struck down so low. I kept saying to myself, "Ain't no way! Ain't no way!" My grandmother held my hand and said, "You'll be all right, son," but I kept looking at Coach Gage and thinking, "Ain't no way you treat me like this."

But that awards dinner taught me the lesson of not putting too much emphasis on individual awards and to stay focused on team goals. And since that day, I always have. I try to look at the big picture. Personal awards don't mean anything to me. The two times I cried as a professional basketball player were when we lost the NBA Championship to Houston and when I got traded from the Knicks to the Golden State Warriors in 1998. I never celebrated when I was voted onto the '94 All-Star team, the NBA All-Defensive second-team, or as the Sixth Man of the Year in 1997. Only when my team lost and I got traded from the team and the city I loved playing for did I shed tears.

A far more disturbing incident happened years later when I was 15. My Auntie Anita and my cousin Shelly were murdered by Shelly's husband, a guy named Willie Hill. They were both beautiful women, and he was crazy because Shelly was going to leave him. I remember being in my grandmother's house when Antonio came running in yelling, "Man, Willie just killed Anita and Shelly."

We ran down to her house, but the police were already there and they wouldn't let us in. I remember standing out there and crying for a long time. It was the first time I ever experienced the death of someone I loved. It was shocking and it really hurt.

A couple of years after the shootings of Anita and Shelly, I had a gun in my hands for the first time. I was working at a store called R&R after school, and this older kid who worked there with me laid the gun that he kept on top of the counter. I grabbed it and put my hand on the trigger and said to him, "Man what are you doing with a little fake gun?"

"Man, that gun ain't fake," he said. "You better look at the bullets inside it."

I still didn't believe him. I was about to pull the trigger thinking it was fake. This kid was the type of kid who was always laughing, but his face all of a sudden got stone serious. I was pointing the gun at myself, that's how crazy I was. I opened the gun up at the last moment just to look at the bullets and I saw that they were real. I put that gun down and broke into a cold sweat.

"Man, I almost blew my head off," I said.

CHAPTER 4

A MODERN-DAY WILL ROGERS

"I never met a man I didn't like."

—Will Rogers, American cowboy humorist,
part Cherokee Indian and native Oklahoman

After I graduated from Burroughs Elementary School, I was bused to Madison Middle School in West Tulsa. I knew what kind of school it was—Monty had gone there and told me that the Ku Klux Klan used to burn crosses on the railroad tracks across the street from the Ziegler Park football field where the school played its games. The ratio of whites to blacks at Madison was 70 to 30 percent. This shocked me. I really didn't see a lot of white folks growing up, and I'd never seen so many white kids in one place before.

The first day, I was very anxious. A white kid came and knocked my book off my desk and onto the floor and started laughing. He was looking at his friend who was laughing, too. I asked him to pick the book up and he said, "I ain't picking it up, nigger." Man, that just sent me off. I exploded and beat the kid up and the principal suspended me. The kid who started it got away scot-free.

I walked into the principal's office and said, "It's not fair that I'm getting punished and the other kid's getting away with it."

But he just said, "I don't agree with what you did. You're the one who threw the first punch."

It was the middle of the day so I asked him, "I don't have a way to get back home now. Can I wait until school is out so I can take the school bus with everybody else?"

"No," he said, "you have to leave school grounds now."

I wasn't sure where I was because I'd never been in that part of West Tulsa before. I wasn't going to call my mother or my grandmother to see if they'd come pick me up because I knew I'd get a whupping for it.

I had a dollar and something like sixty cents in my pocket so I caught a bus and just started riding. I'd never ridden a bus that far all by myself before. It was only about a 15-mile ride, but I got on the wrong bus going in the wrong direction. Instead of going north I went south because I set my sights on the biggest building downtown, the Williams Center, and I used that as my guide. It seemed like I was traveling forever. When the bus finally dropped me off at the Williams Center, I only had enough change for one more bus fare.

I was a quiet kid, reluctant to ask a lot of questions. I just went on hunches I had and tried to make it back on my own. I didn't want to have to tell the story to one of my brothers or friends and have them think I wasn't smart enough to find my way back home. I was very proud and that hurt me at times.

For example, I was too proud to complain about my shoes. My feet had grown faster than any of my brothers; I was the only one besides Lynn who grew to be eventually more than six feet tall. So when I wore Tony and Monty's hand-me-downs, they were too small and I got corns on my feet. But instead of telling anybody—I knew my mother didn't have the money to buy me new shoes—I just wore their shoes and suffered.

I jumped on this bus called the Super Loop—it looped around the perimeter of Tulsa—and I ended up getting off on Peoria Street, probably only 20 blocks from where we were living then. But again, instead of walking north, I headed back south, because I still had my eyes set on the Williams Center downtown. Once I got my mind set on something, I didn't let up.

When I hit Denver Street, there was a dry cleaners shop on the corner that I recognized, and I finally found my way back home. The principal suspended me from school for three days, but I didn't tell my mother that. Each day I just acted like I was going to school and I waited until she left home for work and then I walked back home. When I did go back to Madison, the kid I got into the fight with never bothered me again, in fact, he turned out to be an alright person down the road. He saw—as did everyone else in the class—that you couldn't mess with me. He saw that and he respected it.

My basketball coach at Madison was Bob Hunt, and he was the first coach I ever loved. He was a really good man. He knew that the other black kids on the team and I didn't have much money and had to take the bus to and from school every day, so he would have big meals at his house for the entire team and pick us up in North Tulsa and then drive us all home. I'd never befriended a white person before him. I didn't think until then that whites and blacks could co-exist. He was the first white man I met who treated me kindly and made me realize that there are good people of every race.

I became friends with his son, Richie Hunt, who also played on the team, and I remember one day when he and I and a cou-

ple of our teammates were walking over to Richie's house after a
practice and one of us yelled out at these high school kids driving
by in a car, "Fuck you, peckerwoods. Aaah!"

Everyone except Richie and I ran away. We stood our
ground. We weren't the one who had yelled anything. The high
school kids got out of the car and they were some big-ass white
dudes.

One of them said, "Who in the hell said that?" And he
pointed at me. "You say that?"

"I didn't say that stuff to you all," I said. "I wasn't the one
who said it."

He said, "You better not have said it."

"I didn't," I said, "and I ain't running. Whatever goes down,
goes down."

Richie didn't budge either. He stood right with me and that
taught me a very valuable lesson, one that until then I wouldn't
have ever thought possible. Richie was my friend, but he was
white, too, and the fact that he was going to stand with me, a
black kid, and fight against a group of bigger, white teenagers
stunned me. I think they saw there was something special in that,
too, and they got back in their car and left us alone.

Actually, I have Indian blood in me, too. My mother was
one quarter Creek Indian, so I have one-eighth Creek Indian
blood. The Creek Indians settled in Tulsa in 1826. "Tulsy" is a
Creek Indian term meaning "Old Town."

I didn't pay much attention to my Indian ancestry growing
up and neither did my mother. I wish we would've because the
benefits for half-blood Indians were something we should have
taken advantage of. My brothers and sisters and I probably could
have had a more stable environment growing up instead of moving from place to place.

But my mother was born in 1943, and even in the 1970s
and early 1980s, these things were not widely known among
blacks in North Tulsa who had Indian blood in them. And there

were quite a lot of us. As blacks in Tulsa, we had to deal with our fair share of racism.

When we lived on Virgin Street and then again in a house on Marshall Street, both times we were within a few of blocks of historic Greenwood Avenue. They used to call Greenwood Avenue the "Black Wall Street." Black folks in Tulsa were very self-sufficient in the 1920s. They owned a lot of successful businesses, and the white people were jealous of that. The dollar floated around many times before it left the black community. There was a lot of money in Tulsa back then. It was called the "Golden Age" and Tulsa was the oil capital of the world. The black community had its own hospital, police department, everything. It was very upstanding and a model of economic success.

But on May 31, 1921, 35 blocks of black businesses and homes were burned down, including all of Greenwood Avenue. It is still the worst race riot in United States history. As many as 10,000 white men and boys, as well as police officers and a local unit of the National Guard, helped burn the black community down.

The story among blacks was that it started when a black man, a shoeshine boy, was accused of assaulting a white woman, who was an elevator operator. I heard he was in the elevator with the lady and it was just the two of them in there. The elevator jolted and she fell and he caught her. She started screaming, "Rape, rape, rape."

They put him in the city jail and were talking about hanging him, but the black community wasn't going to have that. Mobs of white and black people gathered outside the jail, the whites setting to lynch this black man, the blacks there to defend him. A white man was killed while trying to take a gun out of the hands of a black man and then the violence began.

Three hundred people were killed. The Ku Klux Klan swept through North Tulsa, burning crosses on black people's lawns, marching down the streets in their white robes. Afterwards, the governor of Oklahoma declared martial law and black people were rounded up by the police and the National Guard and put into the Booker T. Washington baseball stadium.

Greenwood Avenue became a shell of itself. When I was a kid, they came and built a highway over it and it killed the community. Older black folks always talked about the Greenwood race riot. Years later, it was still in their minds. In 2000, the Tulsa Race Riot Commission recommended that reparations be paid to the survivors of the riot and their descendants.

When I was growing up, segregation was not too far in the past, so there was still a lot of tension. I knew where I stood as a black kid. I knew to be careful and to handle myself accordingly when I ventured into South Tulsa. We didn't travel as far back then as kids do now without fear of something bad happening. But I remember feeling thankful that I didn't grow up in the generations of my grandmother or mother. It was tough for them to deal with the abuse they had to go through.

My grandmother was born in 1921 and worked 10, 11 hours a day as a caretaker at a nursing home and later at a shelter for abused woman and children. She'd work through the night and sometimes through the next day. I took my mother's energy and my grandmother's hard work and put them together. I never let things affect me, and as I said before, I didn't hold grudges against people. I learned from basketball that you have to learn how to play with different people and you don't look to see what the color of a man's face is when he's open, you just pass him the ball.

Even when she was in her fifties, and even though she was only five foot tall, my grandmother was really into playing sports with her grandchildren. She was aggressive and didn't take any mess from anybody. It didn't matter if you were the president of the United States, she didn't care. When we lived with my grandmother at her house on Elwood Street she always had food and it was a more stable environment.

In the ninth grade at Madison—middle school went all the way through the ninth grade in Oklahoma back then—Coach Hunt decided to retire and the kids from one of the private academies came over to Madison because their basketball program had been dropped. One of the new kids' brother became the freshman basketball coach. I was used to being treated fairly by Coach Hunt, but this coach started his brother and the kids from the Academy over me and my teammates, even though I was better than all of them. So I quit the team. I wasn't going to play the fool and sit on the bench when I knew that I should be on the court playing.

Whenever I strayed away from basketball, I would start doing things like drinking and smoking weed that I would've been better off staying away from. Monty was dealing drugs pretty heavily back then. I would see him out on the streets; he was living on his own by that time. Every once in a while, Monty would hand me a $10 bag of weed.

A friend of mine was into boxing, and I went with him to the gym he worked out in just to watch him. His coach approached me and said, "You ever box before?"

I told him, "I don't like boxing."

"You might start to like it," he said. "Give it a try."

So he put me in the ring against one of his better kids and I just hit this kid four times and he went down to the canvas. I was like, "Oh, man." The coach tried to get me to come down and box again, but I told him, "No, boxing is not for me."

I loved watching boxing, particularly Muhammad Ali, but the sport didn't interest me the way basketball did. I tried a lot of things to see if I liked them. But if anything took away too much time from basketball, I gave it up.

That summer I played a lot of ball again down in the parks, but I skipped playing for the high school team during my sophomore year. I loved the game too much, and I didn't want to play organized ball if a coach was going to ruin it for me. I loved competition. All I did growing up was compete against my brothers. But I missed the camaraderie of having teammates and the success I felt on the basketball court. I missed the excitement and the fans. I missed the roar of the crowd. When I had played in the organized league at Lincoln Park, we drew big crowds and I loved hearing the crowd's roar after a good play. When you're playing in the parks, you're just shooting with a bunch of guys. There's no roar from the crowd.

As a junior at Tulsa Central, Robert Williams, a good friend of mine convinced me to try out for the varsity with him. I made the team, but the coach, whose name was Butch Fisher, told me, "You can either sit on the bench on varsity all year because I've got my players, or you can go down and play on the junior varsity."

I never liked sitting on the bench and I was only five foot six so I went down to the junior varsity team and averaged 17 points per game. I worked out real hard again over the next summer playing ball in the parks and lifting weights and I grew a couple of inches. In my senior year, before the kids on the football team finished their season and began the basketball team season, Coach Fisher named me the starting point guard. I was a student of the game. The Philadelphia 76ers were my team. I loved watching Maurice Cheeks and I modeled my game after his, passing the ball first and thinking of scoring last.

I had a good first game of the season. I didn't have a single turnover. In the last seconds of the game, we were down by one and I was open for a shot so I took it and missed. I had only taken a few shots the entire game, but Coach Fisher jumped all over me.

"Why the hell did you take that shot?" he yelled at me afterward.

We lost the game by one point, and after the game he was all over me again, but I bit my tongue. The very next game the football players came onto the team and Coach Fisher sat me on the bench. I accepted it. We were playing McClain High, our archrivals. I got put in during garbage time. We were getting killed.

Right away I got the ball running out on a fast break. We had this freshman kid on our team who could really jump and as I was getting ready to lay the ball in, I saw this kid charging down the court. I thought I'd please the crowd by giving them something to cheer about so I laid the ball off to this kid. He dunked the ball, but the ref waved off the basket and called me for traveling.

Coach Fisher went off. He pulled me out of the game and started yelling at me, "What the hell are you doing?"

"Coach," I said. "I was going to give the crowd some excitement and let the kid dunk."

The next day in practice I was out on a fast break again and my teammate, who was defending me in the drill, let me go in for the lay-up. Coach Fisher stopped the practice right there and jumped in this kid's face.

"You should have put John's ass on the floor," he yelled. "Don't let anyone come in for an uncontested lay-up."

My teammate said, "He's my teammate. I'm not going to knock him down."

But Coach Fisher just kept yelling, "I don't care who he is. You put his ass on the floor."

I took off my practice jersey and threw it on the court at his feet and started cussing him out.

"All right," I said. "You going to talk noise?"

Then I walked out of the gym and went back and found Monty and told him the story. He came back to the gym with me and started after Coach Fisher. I never saw a man so scared in my life. Coach Fisher was stumbling, trying to back up and Monty was charging him, getting right in his face.

"You ever say anything like that again to my brother," Monty said, inching closer towards Coach Fisher,"and I'm going to kick your butt."

As Monty approached, Coach Fisher backpedaled towards the gymnasium door.

"Now you get your fat butt out of the gym," I yelled as he walked out.

I got kicked off the team, but that incident with Coach Fisher is what drove me from then on. I said to myself, "I'm going to prove to this cat that he made a mistake." And I set out to prove to Coach Fisher that he was wrong about me. At that moment, I committed myself to becoming a basketball player.

I got a job after school. I started working at the *Tulsa World* newspaper company downtown loading papers on slates. I just went down there one afternoon and asked for a job. Both Tony and Monty had worked there. It was very demanding work, stacking papers and then lifting them up in heavy bundles and placing them onto these slates.

I remember taking my checks—I only made about $30 a week—and going down to this store called Globes to get them cashed. I was only 16, so I wasn't old enough to have a bank account. The manager at Globes said he would cash them, but I had to buy something at the store with the money. They had a beautiful leather jacket, and I always wanted one, so I started putting money down for it in November.

Every week, I'd bring my check in and I'm paying and paying down on the jacket and by the time I finally paid it off in full—I think I overpaid for it—it was May. I didn't care. I started wearing it anyway, but it was hot, really hot outside. I was sweating walking around wearing that leather jacket.

In a pick-up game after the basketball season, I went up to that freshman who could jump out of the gym and I asked him, "How do you jump like that?"

His name was Michael Dogan and all the Dogan boys had crazy hops. He told me he did a lot of toe raises. The toe raises were what made him jump so high. I was five foot ten by then, but I still couldn't even dunk a ball on an eight-foot basket. Every night after that, though, I did hundreds of toe raises. I did toe raises until the muscles in my calves screamed.

Then one night playing in the park, I got the ball on a breakaway and instead of just laying it up, I decided to try to dunk. I planted my foot real hard in front of the basket and just exploded up and jammed the ball in on a regulation ten-foot basket. That dunk inspired me to work even harder to become a real solid player. It made me play that much harder and aggressive. Suddenly, I didn't just want to score or lay balls in off the backboard, I wanted to score with authority by dunking.

A friend of mine at the time, Robert Williams, joined the army, but I never thought of joining the army. Although my grades weren't that good and I hadn't played but two games of basketball at Tulsa Central High my senior year, I had this dream of walking on at some college and earning a basketball scholarship. My mother and my grandmother didn't have the money for me to go to college, but I went to a senior orientation at my high school and found out that I could go to a junior college on grants and loans.

I'm not exactly sure why they were fighting, but I believe it was over a girl and that one of them was messing with the other's girlfriend. That's what I heard. When I got outside, it seemed like the entire school was standing around waiting for the fight to occur. That's how fights took place in high school. One kid would say to the other kid he wanted to fight, meet me at this place at this time, and we'll get it on.

The kid I knew, whose girlfriend was fooling around on him, was standing out in the parking lot and there was already a crowd around him when the other kid walked up to him and pulled out a knife. The kid broke out of the crowd and started running and as he was being chased by the kid with the knife, he pulled out a 22-caliber gun and shot the kid with the knife twice in the chest.

Everybody fled the scene, running this way and that, screaming. But I stood there and watched this kid stumble to his death. It shocked me to witness this happening before my own eyes. Later on that night, my friend, Robert Williams, and I got together to talk about what happened, and what we were going to do with our lives. I knew that I was glad to be saying goodbye to high school.

CHAPTER 5

WALKING ON THE WILD SIDE

"No one around here knew what he had because he wasn't John Starks yet."

—Jimmie Tramel, basketball writer for the *Tulsa World*

During my senior year after I quit the team, I hung out a lot with two friends of mine named Daniel Cephus and Robert Williams. We used to drink a lot of wine and beer and smoke weed and then go out and steal cars. I looked at it as a way to make money and buy things that I couldn't have had otherwise.

Malibus and Capris were very popular cars back then, and we would bend the windows all the way back and reach an arm in and pop open the lock. Then we'd snap the steering wheel lock, stick a screwdriver in the ignition, pop the lock and start the car up and drive off.

We'd steal the "Trues" spoke rims and stereo systems and sell all them for $300 to $400. That was a lot of money for a kid in high school. I can remember once Robert drove Daniel and I down to Oklahoma City where we stole a car and then drove it back to Tulsa, taking the back roads because we figured the police would be looking for the car out on the highway. It took us two and a half hours and I drove, because I felt safer that way. I need to be in control of the situation, I knew I wouldn't do anything crazy. I trusted myself to get back home safely.

Twice we almost got caught. Once in an apartment complex, we had just broken into this car and were getting ready to pop the steering wheel when this man and woman walked out. They were standing in front of the car and even though we tried to duck down in our seats, they saw us.

Daniel said to me, "I'm going to open this door and you be right behind me."

The car had a gearbox sticking up right in the middle of the two seats, but I told Daniel, "I'll be right behind you. You don't even have to worry."

He opened that door and jumped out and I hopped right over the gearshift and was right out the door and on his heels in a second. We both tore right out of there.

Another time we were driving a stolen car when the police crept right by us. I stopped the car by the side of the road and we both jumped out and took off. Afterward, I said to myself, "Man, what are you doing? What are you doing? I've got to stop doing this."

I knew I wasn't going to be a life-long criminal, but I was like a lot of kids who grow up not having a lot of things. Some way, you go out and try to provide for yourself. Stealing cars and later, selling weed, that's what I did.

A year later when I was in junior college, Daniel died in a stolen car with the police chasing him. He hit Apache Hill in North Tulsa going 90 miles per hour and just flew right off it and crashed from what was told to me. He must have been high, because if he were conscious of the steepness of Apache Hill and how fast he was going, I'm pretty sure he would've slowed that car down.

Daniel wasn't a bad kid. He stole cars because it was something he could do to make money. He was good at it. He was a nice kid. He'd give you the shirt off his back. Daniel came from a foster home. He was a hell of a football player at Tulsa Central. He probably could've made it as a scholarship football player in college if he had worked at it. I knew what kind of person he was, and it really hurt me that he died that way. He was just a kid trying to survive.

His death really froze me. I used to break out into a cold sweat thinking, "That could've been me in that car." I was close, closer than I wanted to be, to being in that car with Daniel. Desperate, running from the cops, no way out, nowhere else to go.

I enrolled in the fall of 1984 at Rogers State College in Claremore, Oklahoma and tried out for the basketball team, but the coach already had a set squad, so I was placed on the taxi squad. If one of the players on the regular team got injured, kicked off or quit, I would receive his spot. But before that occurred I ended up getting kicked out of the school.

I was living in the dorms on campus with the other basketball players when this kid down the hall kicked in the door of the dorm room I lived in with two other guys. This kid, who was also a basketball player, got drunk one night and decided to vent his anger over something on our door. The dean of the college said that any damage to the room was our responsibility and would go on our tab.

We told the kid, "We're not going to pay for this darn door. You're going to pay for it." Still, he wouldn't ante up for it.

We had been in his room and seen that he had some very nice stereo equipment in there. They had a big old boom box. I said to my roommates, "Y'know what, I've got an idea how we can get this all paid for. We'll fix his butt."

We devised a plan to break into their room during a basketball game and take the boom box. Since my roommates and I didn't suit up for games and just sat in the stands watching, we would sneak out during the game and go back to the dorm and take the equipment. The night before the game, while I was hanging out in their room, I unlocked their window.

It all worked to plan, I climbed in through their window, took the stereo and one of my roommates had a car so we drove to my cousin Michael's house in Tulsa about 30 miles away and stashed the stereo. Then we came back to the game like nothing happened. When the game was over, we all walked back to their room and they opened their door and looked in and said, "Man, somebody stole our stuff."

I was like, "Aw man, that's messed up. That's really too bad."

We were clowning with them. I was planning to give the box back, but I wanted to make them stew because I was so pissed off that the guy who kicked in our door wasn't going to pay for it.

But then they reported the theft to security and the college did an investigation asking everyone in the dorm if they knew anything about it and they came to the conclusion that we had something to do with it.

I said, "What are you talking about? We were at the game." They said, "No, you left the game."

I was a huge Perry Mason fan. So I knew they couldn't prove anything without the evidence. The police came and took us all down to the station and I said to my two roommates, "Look here, do not say anything. They can't prove nothing. So don't say nothing. This is our story and we're going to stick by it so stick by it."

So they got us in there and it was funny. It was just like what you see on television. They put us in separate rooms and don't you know, the one guy who was really scared—he was a real country boy, from deep in the country—said, "I didn't do it." He was crying, singing the song. They took us out and my other friend said to me, "I think he told on us."

I told him, "Man, whatever you do, stick to the story. Stick to the story. Don't say a word."

But he got in there and sure enough, he, too said that we all had stolen the stereo. The police came out and told me, "We're going to put you in jail for five years."

I said, "I don't know what you're talking about."

So my two roommates ended up squealing us out. One of them took the police right to my cousin's house and they picked up the stuff and came back and the police chief told me, "We went to your cousin's house and got the stuff."

I wasn't budging. I said, "I still don't know what you're talking about. I had nothing to do with that."

They kept all of us in jail overnight and then we went in front of the judge the next morning. During the whole interrogation, the police told us that they were going to throw all of us in jail, but the prosecutor came in and said, "We want to let them"—pointing at my two roommates—"out on their own personal recognizance without bail, but we want to hold him"—pointing at me—"with a $5,000 bond."

I said, "What you talking about, man?"

The prosecutor ignored me and told the judge that my two roommates should be set free because they were cooperating, but I should be kept in jail. But the judge said, "Just because he won't cooperate doesn't mean he shouldn't get the same deal as the two men who committed the theft along with him." So he let me out, too.

I transferred to Northern Oklahoma in Tonkawa for the second semester, but I had to go back to Claremore for the trial six months later. My roommates received probation and I got five days in the Claremore Jail. I had to tell my coach at Northern,

Ron Brown, that I had to return to Claremore during spring break and serve the time.

Now I was scared to death! I'd never served time behind bars before. I was only 19 years old. They had one man in the county jail who was a mass murderer, he'd killed three or four people and this had been a national story. He was locked in his own separate cell.

I didn't take a shower the first few days I was in there. They put me in a big, old holding tank with 20 other guys. I remember my mother driving me down to the county jail. She was a tough woman and had seen people she knew and loved put into penitentiaries before. She understood.

"I'll tell you, son," she said. "This is not the kind of life you want to live. This is not what you want to do. I'll drop you off here and be back to pick you up in a week, but you think about your life while you're in there."

I walked into the jail on my own and I was nervous. I took the top bunk because I always took the top bunk at home with my brothers. I thought I'd see some big, strong cats in there, but once I looked around, I realized that I was bigger and taller than most of the other guys in the holding tank. The only good thing about the whole experience is that the warden and the guards knew I was young and a college student so they gave me work detail so I could get out of the cell a bit and not be locked up 23 hours of the day. I got to take a shower alone then, too.

I served food to everyone in the jail. So I got out of the cell for an extra hour. When I served the tray of food to the mass murderer—Oh man, that was scary—I almost spilled it all over him.

But when he opened the window for me to pass the food through to him, he didn't look crazy to me. He had calm eyes. I thought he'd be a scary, wild-looking guy, but he looked normal to me.

One thing I found out about jail life is that when you serve the food, you're the most popular guy in the joint. I was the man because I was handing out the food.

I thought, "I'm cool in here. I'm in charge of the food."

The other prisoners would say to me, "Man, give me a little extra," and I obliged because it wasn't my food, it was the city's food.

After I spent my time in jail and got out, I told myself, "This is something I never, ever, ever want to see again, the inside of a jail cell. This is not for me."

I went back to school at Northern Oklahoma to play on the basketball team. Two friends of mine, Darryl Madden and Troy Pettit were going to Northern Oklahoma and they asked me to come down and try out for the team with them. The coach there, Ron Brown, asked me if I could play and I said, "Yeah, I can play." He put me up against one of the guys already on the team in a game of one on one, and after I schooled the guy, Coach Brown said I had a scholarship.

I liked the coach a lot. Over the first 14 games of the season, I was averaging 11 points per game. But after one game, in which I played my best game of the season, I got caught smoking pot in my dorm room. There were two other teammates with me in the room and we created quite a cloud of pot smoke. The resident assistant, a student in charge of our dorm, enlisted the campus police and they looked like a S.W.A.T team when they charged into our room. We had forgotten to put the lock on our door. Everyone on our floor smoked weed, so I don't know why they chose to bust in on us.

My canister of weed was sitting out on the table when they came through the door. The resident assistant yelled out, "You're all going to see the dean about this tomorrow, and he's going to kick you out of school."

I said, "Man, you got us."

I took full responsibility for the possession of the marijuana since I had already made my mind up that if something like this happened, I wouldn't stress out about it. I'd just blow it off. Plus, one of the other guys in the room was from Detroit and he was really upset, saying, "I can't go home because of this. My mother is going to kill me.

I told him, "Listen man, don't even worry about it. You tell the dean when you meet with him that you weren't smoking. You were just in the room, and I was the only one smoking and I'll tell him the exact same thing."

He looked at me startled and said, "You know, he's going to kick you out of school." And I said, "Don't even worry about it."

Coach Brown told me he was sorry that I had to take the rap, but I told him, "Don't worry about it. I was waiting to go, anyway." I just accepted the situation. When I met with the dean, he wanted me to squeal on the other two guys, but I told him that I was the only one smoking the weed. I took the bus back from Tonkawa to Tulsa and had to call up my mother to tell her I was coming home. That was a hard call to make.

I moved in with my brother in a house he owned on Tecumseh Street. My whole family, my mother, brothers and sisters, were living there at the time, too, because they were about to move out to Sacramento. I was very down on myself. Things were looking pretty bleak. Monty was selling a lot of cocaine at the time, seriously dealing, kicking it, rolling in the dough.

I had lived with Monty during my senior year of high school, too. He used to give me dime bags of weed—which you're supposed to get ten joints out of—but I'd roll my joints so tight that I got 20 or 30 joints. Monty used to say to me, "Man, you're as cheap as all outdoors." But I sold them for $1 a joint.

It was a tough time being out of ball. I was down, feeling low. Instead of seeing myself in the NBA, I was wondering, "Will

I ever stop struggling?" I was experiencing hard times. I couldn't dream about tomorrow.

I would get up in the morning, smoke weed and wait for Monty to come and get me—he'd be up most of the night out selling dope—and we'd go to the gym in O'Brien Park. We played games against guys who were playing at Division I schools and I started to dominate. There was something inside of me even then telling me not to let go of the game, to keep my focus on improving my skills. I wouldn't let go. I just kept working, working, working at it. Every morning I'd get up and smoke weed and then Monty and I would go to the gym and play ball. Just doing it again, again and again.

I loved playing playground ball. It's pure basketball with no referees; you call your own fouls. You get into a lot of squabbles over calls because you don't want to lose. There are 50 guys on the sidelines waiting to play, and you know if you lose you're going to be sitting down for the next eight games. It makes for a lot of bad calls, but hard play. It develops toughness, a mental toughness and the park game is a lot more physical game. Even after I started playing for the Knicks I would still go play in the parks in Tulsa.

Playing park ball developed the hunger in me that I needed to get to the NBA. The NBA season is a very grueling, draining season and if a player doesn't have experience playing game after game, like I did in the parks, hour upon hour, then he's not going to have the mental toughness to play in the NBA. You can't be soft and be a dominant park player. A lot of coaches recruit the kid out of the hood who's been through a lot of park ball because they know that kid knows how to survive and win.

The problem with some playground players is that they think the game is all about them. I always had an appreciation for the game and what it took to win. I didn't have a big ego thinking it was O.K. for my team to lose if I scored 40 or 50 points.

Some guys are happy with that, but I always had my sights set on winning, even if it meant that I had to adjust my game.

Monty moved into a house further north on 46th street, and I used to stay with him from time to time, when my mother got ready to move out to Sacramento with the family. I met my wife, Jackie, for the first time at a birthday party my brother Bucky was having at Monty's house. Her cousin lived in a house next door to us. I remember having seen Jackie once before when I played for Northern Oklahoma against Seminole Junior College. She had been a cheerleader for Seminole.

I liked that she was tall and had a track body; she had run the 200 meters in high school and had played basketball. She is a very beautiful woman, but down to earth since she grew up in the country in Wetumka, Oklahoma. I was a little shy, but we talked a lot and I felt comfortable with her. I met her on winter break, but we didn't start dating until three months later when I had moved back to Tulsa after getting kicked out of Northern. Jackie's cousin told her where I was staying and they both came knocking at the door. She knocked on the door and I opened it and Jackie said, "Hi, you remember me?" We went to grab a bite at the Taco Mayo and started to get to know each other better.

It was also at one of Monty's parties that I walked into his room and found him free-basing cocaine. I'd noticed that he was losing weight, but I was shocked to see him smoking cocaine. He saw up close how people just lost all their willpower once they got hooked on cocaine. After selling the stuff, I never thought he would get hooked on it himself. But when I saw that he was smoking it out of a pipe like real heavy users, I knew that he must be hooked, too.

Every night I went to work at the Safeway. I worked there for one year. I started out as a checkout cashier and I was a hard worker. If a can was out of place on one of the shelves in the store, I'd turn it around. One of my older co-workers said to me, "You need to slow down."

But the manager liked that he didn't have to tell me to do something, I kept busy. One day he said to me, "You look like you can lift boxes. Maybe you want to work the night shift and make a couple of dollars more an hour." So he made me a stock person. I stocked all night while the store was closed. My shift was 11 P.M. to 8 A.M. with a break at 4 A.M. That was a good little job. It paid $6 an hour. It was pretty much a hard-working group of people. I listened to a couple of guys who had been there ten to 15 years. I got their perspectives on life and what their jobs meant to them and what hard work was. I took that to heart.

While I was stocking the food on the shelves, I used to jump and touch the beams in the back of the store. They were about 10 1/2 feet off the ground and I used to bet the guys that I could touch them and make a little extra change. One night the lift dropped on my foot and I thought I had broken my toe. But it was just bruised. The manager was real nice to me for a while after that because he thought that I was going to sue the store. There was nothing wrong with working there, but I told myself, "No way I can do this the rest of my life."

Around that time there was a lot of crazy stuff going on, mainly with my family. After Ju Ju had surgery on his foot, he became hooked on cocaine, too, and then when he went with my mother and sisters to Sacramento, he started hanging out with gangs. He was in the eleventh grade at the time, not going to school and hanging out with gangs.

My mother left me her 1976 Chevy Impala when they moved. When I lived with Monty I slept with a gun under my pillow. All kinds of people would knock on Monty's door coming to buy weed and cocaine. I wanted to know why cocaine was so powerful that Monty, Bucky and Ju Ju were all addicted to it so I decided to try it myself. I wanted to know why it made them do the crazy things that it did. So I said to myself, "Let me try this."

Before I went off to work one night, Monty gave me vial of cocaine to snort. I took a couple of snorts of it, and then I remember I went to work. At work I felt real hyper. Stocking the shelves, I was jumping up trying to touch the lights on the ceiling. The cocaine gave me this crazy energy, but before I snorted it, I told myself, "I'm going to make sure this stuff doesn't take me over." I snorted cocaine that one night, but I never did snort it again. I already felt lost, and I didn't want to add any fuel to the fire.

That summer I played in the "Pigs Pop-Off" tournament for the first time. There was also a tournament called Po Bill's World Famous Basketball Classic that was held in Dallas a week before this tournament. We used to bring a few teams down to Dallas from Tulsa and they'd bring a few teams up from Dallas and Houston. A lot of NBA players at the time would play, such as Karl Malone, Moses Malone, Rodney McCray, Jerome Whitehead and Allan Levell.

I was 20 years old and playing against NBA players, and I was holding my own. They named an All-Star team at the end of the tournament and I was named to the Tulsa team along with Wayman Tisdale and Anthony Bowie, two of Tulsa's best players at the time, who were big-time players at the University of Oklahoma.

Monty took notice of it, but I didn't pay it any mind. To me it was just an individual honor, and as I said, I didn't pay attention to personal awards. But Monty said, "Listen man, you're making the All-Star team along with guys who are going to be playing in the NBA in a couple of years. Man, you're going around here dunking on people, killing them, you need to get your butt back in school." I was kind of lost—living a crazy life—and Monty was speaking some knowledge into me to make a choice: keep doing the same thing or make a change for the better.

CHAPTER 6

TIME TO SHINE

"You read about this kind of story about a good person making it good. He did it by fighting and scrapping all the way, it's kind of like the American dream."

—Leonard Hamilton, current Florida State basketball
coach and John Starks's coach at Oklahoma State

I ended up enrolling in Tulsa Junior College in the summer of 1986, but not to play basketball—they didn't even have a team. I wanted to get a business degree so that I wouldn't have to work a manual labor job for the rest of my life. Working at the Safeway had given me more of an appreciation for getting a college education and my grandmother had told me, "John, I don't see you as someone who's going to wind up on the streets. I always see you behind a desk, in an office somewhere." When my grandmother spoke it was like God Almighty, so that stuck with me and I took it to heart.

How I got back on track to playing basketball in college is a bit of a miracle. Monty remembers those times better than I do.

Monty:

John came home from Northern Oklahoma with the notion that he was going to quit school. I was living on Tecumseh Street in North Tulsa and selling drugs. I had dropped out of Northeastern State University because in the first semester I had gotten like four F's and two D's. I'd played on the football team and we had made it to the NAIA national championship game, but I didn't give a shit about being in school. There was too much money to be made out on the streets.

I felt guilty about John getting kicked out of school, because I was the one who had given him the bud that he was smoking when the school officials found him. I gave him $50 and a bag of weed. I felt if he had some money to buy food with and some weed to smoke, he'd be all right. I didn't want to see him quit school like I had. I didn't want to see him make the mistake that I had. I took him up to school one week and he came back the next week saying he got caught with the weed. I thought, "Oh, my God, Granny's going to kill me."

The very next morning after John came home, I woke him up at 8 a.m., and took him down to the Morningstar projects where we used to live and where I had set up shop selling crack. I wanted to show him my side of life. He had this notion that he would make money by selling dope just like me. I told him that I was going to show him what he had to do, that he had to stay down there for the entire day. He had to watch people smoke the dope he sold them and then do anything to get another hit. How they would cry, beg, go out and steal, all of that, just so they could get another hit of the stuff he was selling them.

I sat up there and showed John what it takes to sell drugs. Smokers would come up to me and cry, "Monty, please," and I'd tell them, "I've got your life in my hands. You'd do anything for this stuff." I was showing John what it was like. What he would have to face on a daily basis.

John was down there for one day and he decided after that that he didn't have the heart for selling cocaine. He could sell a little bud, but once he saw what was involved in selling hard drugs, he couldn't do it. He thought it would be easy because he saw all the money I was making.

(But what I was thinking in my mind is that if I got caught I would probably spend the rest of my life in prison. I didn't like that idea.—J.S.)

We started playing ball every day at O'Brien Park on 58th Street and Lewis in the deep north. John had a great jump shot, but I showed him that I could stop him from going to the basket. He was about four inches taller than me, but I weighed about 40 pounds more than him and I told him, "You're not going to win no games shooting jump shots." We'd play games of one on one, and I could bust him ten out of ten games. I was a football player, but I would stop him, foul him, knock him to the ground.

When I blocked his shot, I'd come down on him and pound him. I wouldn't try to hit the ball, I was trying to grab skin. Anything to get him to the point where he developed the attitude of: "Yeah, I'm getting fouled, but I'm still going to make this shot." I was rough with him day after day, letting him get to eight points and then taking him down low and punishing him. When I fouled him, I'd say, "It's my ball. I'm taking it." I would just take everything because I was Big Brother. Pounding it into him, pounding it into him.

I could see him progressing. He quit laying the ball in on lay ups and went in and dunked it. He had been going all the way to the hole, getting his elbow above the rim and then trying to lay the ball in and he'd miss the lay up. I said, "That stuff ain't happening any more. You need to go in there and start dunking." He started letting his heart take over and being more aggressive, getting the attitude of, "I'm not going to let no man beat me."

He'd walk off the court after we played the five-on-five, full-court games and I'd throw the ball at him and yell, "Get your butt back on this court. Don't go nowhere! You don't walk off this court." And we'd go right back at it, playing ten games of one on one to 11 before we stopped for the day. John was 19 years old and I would tell him, "You're not going to be able to go to the next level until you can beat me. If you beat me, you can beat anybody."

John would leave the court after our one-on-one games with cuts and scratch marks all down his arms. That's how I played. If I fouled you, I was going to get my money's worth, just like Charles Oakley used to when he played for the Knicks. Oak was a man. I liked the way Oak played. If he fouled, he fouled hard. And that's the way I played with John.

We used to do fundamental drills, defensive slide drills, shoot jumpers. I'd run the ball down for John for hours and pass him the ball as he come around a fake pick, get his feet set, shooting with no dribble, just catch and shoot. I coached him to get to where he wanted to go and he kept me off the streets.

Anthony Bowie and Wayman Tisdale were playing in these summer pickup games and I told John, "Hey, you're just as good as them." Then all kinds of NBA players started coming in from Texas to play in the Pigs Pop-Off tournament at Booker T. Washington High School, and we were winning the tournaments with just average guys from Tulsa. John was dominating. There would be big crowds of black people at the games, Northside crowds. It was like our Rucker League, and the players took it real serious.

The first time John went up against Dennis Rodman in a tournament game, Rodman was still a senior at Southeast Oklahoma State, but he had a big name in Tulsa already. In the first half, John wasn't playing his normal game. He was passing the ball off, not being aggressive. So at halftime, I chewed him out.

"You're playing like a little punk," I told him. "You're acting like you're scared of him."

In the second half, John came out and busted Rodman's ass for 20 points. He killed him, scoring 27 points for the game. That's when basketball people started talking about John Starks in Tulsa. He never had a nickname down in the playground. He didn't need one. It was always just John Starks.

I knew John was ready when he dunked on Bowie at Amos T. Hall. John had stolen the ball and was on a breakaway when Bowie came down the other side. John went up to dunk with his right hand and Bowie, who was 6-6, went up to block it. John switched up to his left and smashed it. The whole North side knew he was rockin'. After that dunk, I said to him, "Time to shine."

I felt my job was done. There wasn't any more I could do because John was already beating me in one on one. That dunk was like the nail in my coffin. My days of beating him were over.

I called my uncle Mike Mims who was a coach with the University of Oklahoma's basketball team. He had also coached Wayman Tisdale at Booker T. Washington High School. He said he couldn't get John a scholarship at OU and that John should look to go to a smaller school first. I told John, "You got to get back in school and stay there. You can't quit. You're going to do something with your skills. You're not going to be like me."

That was my theme. "I don't want you to have to deal drugs like me!"

I really started getting confidence when I played against Karl Malone and Rodman in the Pigs Pop-Off. Karl was in the NBA and Rodman was a star at Southeast Oklahoma State. Rodman and I later became the only two American NBA players with no varsity high school basketball experience (Dennis didn't play at all in high school and I played in only those two varsity games) to play in an NBA All-Star game. Rodman was a clean-cut kid back then.

Later, when I finally played for Utah in the NBA, I used to listen to the stories Karl told about coming from a little town in

Louisiana, Sommerville. His mother used to strap the ropes to the plow on his and his brother's shoulders and they'd pull it across the fields. I got an appreciation for the work he had put in to achieve playing in the NBA. Listening to Karl's stories made me feel like I had experienced similar hard times. I wasn't handed anything either.

Monty had brought out the will in me. Monty taught me how to play hard on every play the way a football player does. He instilled in me the will to go over the top of players and dunk the ball. I had always had a big-brother syndrome when it came to competing against Monty, like Michael Jordan had with his older brother initially and Serena Williams with Venus. But once I got past that psychological hold, I started beating his butt every time we played, and that meant as much to me as holding my own against the pro players in the Pigs Pop-Off games did.

CHAPTER 7

WEDDING NIGHT RIM-ROCKER

"It was our wedding night, but I asked him if he wanted to play and he said, 'I'd like to play.' So we got into his car and drove to Independence, Kansas."

—Jackie Starks, John's wife

started playing intramural basketball at Tulsa Junior College where I enrolled, and I was scoring around 40 points a game. Usually college scouts don't attend intramural games looking for players, but I had made a little bit of a name for myself from the Pigs Pop-Off tournaments, and this young guy, Tim Bart, who was enrolled as a student at the college and coached my intramural team, knew Ken Trickey Jr., who was the son of Ken Trickey, a basketball coaching legend in Oklahoma.

Bart told me, "I'm going to be a college coach." And I said, "I'm going to be in the NBA." Bart went to his friend, Ken Trickey Jr., because Ken Trickey, who had coached at Oral Roberts in Tulsa for a lot of years and who was just then starting

up the program at Oklahoma Junior College in Tulsa, was looking for players. Ken Trickey Jr. put Bart in touch with his father
and Bart told him, "I've got a guy who can play. I got a stud for
you."

Trickey was originally from Tennessee and he had a pipeline
of players from Chicago and Tennessee from his Oral Roberts
days, but still he was interested.

"Who is he?" Trickey asked.

"John Starks," Bart said.

"Who?" Trickey said.

So Trickey came down to see me play an intramural game
and I scored 50 points. On one play I was just clowning around
at the free-throw line and I threw the ball off the backboard and
I ran up and dunked it. That got his attention and he invited me
down to the tryouts at McClure Park where there were more than
100 players competing to make his OJC team. Monty brought
me down there and Trickey put me on the court against all the
guys he had brought in from Tennessee and Chicago. I held my
own in a big way. Oklahoma Junior College paid for my books
and tuition fees, and that's all I needed, because I had moved in
with Jackie by then and she was working at The Bank of
Oklahoma.

We lived in the Sand Dollar Apartments on Riverside and
61st, right alongside the Arkansas River. We didn't tell Jackie's
folks that we were living together so whenever her mother and
father would come up for the weekend, I'd pack up all my
belongings and put them in the trunk of the Impala. I think they
knew we were living together, but we were just being respectful.

Even though I was one of the most dominating players on
the team, Trickey didn't start me right away. At the start of the
season, he had me sitting on the bench. Monty came to every
game with my grandmother. He would leave her up in the stands
and come up behind the bench and cuss Coach Trickey out for

not playing me. He'd be yelling, "Get my brother in the game." He wasn't going to let me die on the end of the bench. I didn't say much. I knew eventually Coach Trickey would have to play me and when he did I was going to make the most of the time I received.

Monty:
I went and sat with the president of OJC in the stands and told him, "They're not going to blackball my brother. Coach Trickey has to put him in the game."

But still he wouldn't play him. I was going off. Then when John would get in the game, he'd bring the team back from 15 points down to five points down. I'd yell to John, "Steal the ball and go down and dunk it," and John would steal the ball and go the length of the court and rip it. I'd yell, "Steal the ball and do a 360," and Boom! He'd do it. Then Coach Trickey would pull him out of the game and put his own guys back in like they were the ones who brought the team back.

I was sitting on the bench until we went up to this tournament in Boise, Idaho. We were playing against Dennis Johnson's little brother Joey Johnson. I forget the team he played on, but he held records for the high jump in Idaho. From a standstill jump underneath the basket, he could get his shoulders up above the rim. On one play, I caught him flat-footed and I jumped from a standstill under the basket and slammed the ball in with my elbow above the rim.

We were getting blown out and Trickey took me out of the game, but after the game, on the plane ride home, he came up to me and asked me if I thought I could play the point guard position. I said, "Just put me in the game," After that, I got a lot more playing time and we took off.

Coach Trickey taught me a lot. I have a great deal of respect for him. He is one of those coaching "lifers." Oral Roberts re-hired him after he coached at Oklahoma Junior College and now he's 77, and still coaching high school basketball in Muskogee. He is the winningest coach in ORU history. Trickey was a real go-getter. He'd rather get a kid off the streets than a kid who had everything.

Before one game I was reading the program and I saw that they had listed me as six foot five. I went up to coach and told him, "I'm not 6-5. I'm only 6-2. We've got to get this changed."

Coach Trickey looked at me and said, "Be quiet. You're going to thank me one day." And he was right.

I wasn't dreaming about the NBA at that point, I was dreaming about getting a scholarship to a Division I school. But Tricky told me, "Son, I've seen a lot of pro players and coached guys who went pro like Anthony Roberts at ORU, and you have a chance to be just as good as all of them." Anthony Roberts had played four seasons for the Denver Nuggets, but died later of a gunshot wound.

I got married to Jackie on December 13, 1986 in a small church in West Tulsa. We were supposed to play in Independence, Kansas that night, but no one, especially me, knew about it. Everyone thought the game had been canceled.

At five o'clock, Tim Bart, our assistant coach, was running all over Tulsa, pulling guys out of malls, the parks, the dorms. He got all the players except me into a van, ready for the two and a half hour drive from Tulsa to Independence, Kansas, when Coach Trickey asked him, "Where's John Starks?"

"Coach, don't you know," Bart said. "John got married this afternoon."

Coach Trickey called me at the wedding reception—I didn't know how he tracked me down, this was long before cell phones—and told me we had a game that night. I said, "Coach, you told me we didn't have one. You assured me we weren't going to play. I just got married."

"Well, we got one," Coach Trickey said. "You think you can make it down, anyway?"

"Coach, come on," I said. "I've got my wedding night."

"Well, fine," he said. "If you can be here, you be here."

So I'm feeling guilty because I'm letting down my team. I told Jackie, "We've got a game in Kansas tonight and Coach Trickey wants me there."

Jackie said, "What do you want to do?"

"I'd like to play," I said.

I've got a very supportive wife. She used to play basketball so she knew about the competitive urge. We cut the wedding reception short and jumped into the car. We took Highway 75 and got there in an hour and 45 minutes, even after a state trooper stopped me along the way and gave me a speeding ticket.

The gym we were playing in had a little tin roof. I ran into the locker room at half time high on adrenaline, the way a kid gets. Some reporter, after I was already playing for the Knicks, wrote that I ripped off my tuxedo when I burst into the locker room. But that part isn't true. I changed into my uniform at the gym. We were getting drilled pretty good, but I barged through the door yelling, "We can beat 'em. We can win this one."

I scored 22 points in the second half, but we still lost. At the end of the game, I took an alley-oop pass from half court like it was a football Monty used to pass me out on Elwood Street and I dunked the ball in backwards, over my head and then hung onto the rim.

Coach Trickey got up off the bench and yelled, "You can just go home if you're gonna act like a fool." He really didn't like it when I hung from the rim. But Tim Bart told me years later that he always remembered that dunk in that little tin building in Independence, Kansas.

"That's just how you were," he said. "You would dunk on anyone. Anyone got in your way, you'd go over the top of him. You didn't care. I remember thinking that night that your life was shaping up like a Hollywood movie, only it was playing out in places like Boise, Idaho and Independence, Kansas."

But I knew there was a danger to being an explosive leaper, too, and thinking you could just dunk the ball whenever you wanted. I knew I had to learn the game fully and not just fall back on my dunking abilities.

Monty told me a few games later into the season that Coach Leonard Hamilton at Oklahoma State was interested in giving me a scholarship even though I only had one more year of NCAA eligibility left. He had just become the coach there and was picking his first recruiting class. Richard Dumas, a six-foot-eight forward from Booker T. Washington High School in Tulsa, who later played for the Phoenix Suns in the NBA, had already committed to Coach Hamilton. It was my dream to play Division I college ball. Monty knew that.

Monty:
When John got to Oklahoma Junior College, he saw for the first time where his skills could take him. I called Leonard Hamilton and got in touch with his secretary and I said, "I got a player down here, my little brother, that I want Coach Hamilton to come down and see. He's averaging 27 points per game at Oklahoma Junior College."

Leonard Hamilton called me back and said, "I'll be down this Friday night to watch your brother play." They were going up against Northeastern A&M College of Miami, Oklahoma and the game was being played in the Expo Sports Center in Tulsa.

All week long I'm telling John, "Now you've got to play. This is it! We're going for the scholarship. This is serious now. It's time for your butt to perform." I was just drilling it into him, getting him pumped up, building his attitude.

I sat next to Coach Hamilton in the stands and I told him, "Coach Hamilton, watch this!" I hollered to John. "Go down and dunk it backwards!" And he was killing them. John had 30-something points. After the game, Coach Hamilton told John, "I can't talk to you, but I can talk to him," meaning me.

I met him at the Red Lobster and he said, "I want John to come to Oklahoma State."

I said, "He can come?"

Coach Hamilton said, "Yes."

But it turned out that Coach Hamilton only had one scholarship left and it came down to this guy playing for Northern Oklahoma, my old school, and me as to who was going to get it. Soon after, we played Northern Oklahoma and Coach Trickey called me into the huddle before the game and as he was going through the lineups he looked at me and said, "Who do you want to stick, John?"

"I got him," I said, meaning the other guy who was up for the scholarship to Oklahoma State with me.

I went out and just thoroughly destroyed this kid. I think he scored two points. I shut him down and dunked on him and straight out destroyed him. Coach Hamilton stopped recruiting the kid after the game.

The summer before I went to Oklahoma State, I had to take 18 credit hours to graduate with my associate's degree in Business Administration. Coach Hamilton told me, "I can't see how you're going to make it." All the courses I'd taken at the other two junior colleges weren't counted. But I had read a line in a philosophy book that really motivated me. I wish I had majored in philosophy. I've always been a big thinker.

Before going to Stillwater with Jackie, I was working out with Monty in the weight room at O'Brien gym and I noticed Monty had this far-away look on his face. He had a whole different attitude, like he wasn't even there so I knew something was up. I hoped he was just nervous.

That night, Jackie and I were watching the news on television when the newscaster said there had been a rash of robberies at a convenient store. The suspect was a solidly built, five-foot-10 black man. I said to Jackie, "I think I know somebody like that." A couple of days later, I got a call from Monty at the Tulsa County Jail saying he'd been arrested.

I was fulfilling a dream by going to play Division I College basketball, but my brother, who was my inspiration, was going to prison. He was sentenced to 18 years in the Lexington State Penitentiary. He'd pushed me to fulfill my dream, and now he wasn't going to be there to share it with me. It was very bittersweet.

When Monty got locked up in the Tulsa County Jail waiting for his trial, he started going through withdrawal. He called me up and asked me if I could bring a bag of weed into him at the jail. I told him I didn't think that would be such a good idea, but he said, "Yeah, you can do it. Yes, you can. They do it all the time. You can do it." He was in a real bad way.

Now I knew that I could be charged with a crime if I got caught. But this was Monty and I did it out of love. I wouldn't have done it for anyone else and I only did it one time. I got some weed and I took it down to the jail along with some papers his lawyer had given me. I talked to Monty in his jail cell through a little window. A guard was looking at us through a mirror up on the ceiling.

Monty asked me, "You bring it?" And I said, "I brought it."

"You see that door down there at the end of the hall?" Monty said. "Walk down there and a guy will open the door a little ways and you just slip him the bag."

I walked down the hall to the door and the door pulled open and I quickly handed the package over to a hand that reached out from behind the door. But just as I handed the package over, a police officer came around the corner and said, "What did you hand through that door?"

Monty came up to the bars of his cell and screamed at the officer, "He didn't do nothing. He didn't do nothing."

Monty was going crazy. He thought he had gotten me caught. I would have lost my scholarship to Oklahoma State and might have gone to jail, too.

"Shut up, Monty," I said, "I got it under control." Then I turned to the officer and showed him the papers I had from Monty's lawyer. "I'm giving my brother the papers I got from his lawyer."

I believe God planted those papers in my hand, because without them, you probably would not have ever heard about John Starks, the NBA player.

Monty:

I tried to keep my drug use away from John. I didn't want him to see me like that. But if I hadn't been home for two or three days, John would come looking for me.

Cocaine was a recreational drug. It was a fad thing back in the '80s. Snort a little coke. "Boy, you're looking good." My cousin left me a three-ounce bag of cocaine and I tried it then and it didn't do anything to me. I put it in a joint of weed and I'd smoke it that way and then more and more. I started craving it. I didn't know what it was doing to me. Nobody knew what it was doing to them.

Soon I'm doing more and more to where I started snorting it and then free-basing it. I just started doing it because all my friends were doing it. It was like an epidemic around Tulsa back then. It wasn't anything to make a couple of thousand dollars in a day around here selling it. That's how many people were doing it in this small a town.

When I was arrested, I felt like I had screwed my life up. I was facing a lot of time. Although I'd never been arrested before, I was sentenced as a habitual criminal. The judge gave me 18 years. Even the way I got caught and charged with armed robbery was screwed up.

I had a friend whose girlfriend ran a store. I used to give him dope and when he'd run up a big tab, we would stage a little robbery at his girlfriend's store. She was in on the whole thing. We did it several times. We had to make it look like a real robbery. You couldn't just go in there and say, "Give me the money," and run. His girlfriend had to look like she wasn't just handing the money over to somebody. The night we got caught, my friend had a b-b gun in his hand and that's how it became armed robbery.

The police had set up a roadblock on the highway between Sand Springs, where the robbery took place, and Tulsa. Someone had tipped them off. My friend was driving and I was in the passenger seat splitting up the money, I was giving him his share minus whatever he owed me, when they stopped us. At the time we got caught, my friend was doing 20 years of parole time. I knew him since grade school, so I told the police that I was the one who had committed the crime.

That first year, they transferred me from the Lexington penitentiary to Stringtown, where in 1988, a big race riot occurred when a couple of Muslim inmates stole some of the Aryan brothers' food out of their lockers. That pissed these guys off and they wanted to kill the Muslim inmates, but the two guys who had committed the robbery were shipped out to McCallister, a maximum security prison.

The white guys didn't know that, they wanted to kill somebody, and that's how the riot started. I was right there. When the Aryan brothers stormed the prison guards and took them hostage, I went and got my knife because if one of them came after me, I had to be able to deal with them. Everyone had a knife in prison. They checked us, but we had our shanks hidden in the ground, all over the place and we were ready to go to war.

The governor sent in the National Guard and when they came through the prison gates, they shot in the air a few times, and said,

"Everyone on the ground!" In two or three days, they took the prison back from the Aryan brothers. They sent us all to McCallister, which had been condemned by the federal government. Four hundred inmates were transferred.

The place was disgusting. It hadn't been occupied for six months. We had rats coming up through the sewers and it was two weeks before we got to take our first cold shower. We ate oranges and peanut butter for breakfast, lunch and dinner for about a week. We had to stay there six months.

They gave me pre-parole after three years in 1989 and I was doing great. I had a job at Pepsico and I was working out and in great shape. John had set it up with his agent for me to come up to New Jersey and get a tryout with the New Jersey Generals of the United States Football League. But because I was on parole, the Oklahoma Parole Board wouldn't let me leave the state. John wrote letters to the Parole Board of Oklahoma to tell them I was going to play football in New Jersey. It was my big chance, but they wouldn't let me cross state lines. Then they sent me back to prison when I came up for mandatory parole because they realized that they had sentenced me wrong by giving me pre-parole too early.

I got out on pre-parole again in 1992 and this time I went right back to the projects where I was used to making my money and set up shop. I felt comfortable there. I didn't have any money and I wasn't going to get a job because I'm always going to do what I want to do. I was walking out of the projects, Osage Apartments, one of the only ones we hadn't lived in growing up since we'd been in Morningstar, Commanche, Seminole Hill and Vernon Manor, when a guy in a car asked me, "Hey, you want a ride, Monty?"

"Yeah, give me a ride over to my grandmother's house," I said. She lived only about a mile and a half away so I was going to walk it, but I got in the car. As soon as he pulled away from the curb about six police cars stopped us. They knew I was a drug dealer and they found a gun underneath the driver's seat. I was on parole so that automatically set me back ten years even though the guy driving the

car came and testified that it wasn't my gun. I was absolutely devastated. I'd been out of jail three months.

They were going to take all of my good-time days away for already having served five years in prison, which meant I would have to re-do them all over again, but then the warden needed me to play in the Cop versus Con football game. It was a big game held every year in Union Stadium in Tulsa between the police and the prisoners in Oklahoma. The warden knew I had been an All-America football player in high school and he wanted to use my name. John was already playing for the Knicks and they wanted to put in the papers, "Vincent Lewis, John Starks's brother, is playing in the Cop versus Con football game."

I told the warden that I wasn't going to play unless they gave me my good-time days back. I had bargaining leverage. He wanted me to play the game because the warden and the police chiefs had a little wager on the outcome of the game. It was like the movie, The Longest Yard *with Burt Reynolds. Also, I told the warden that he couldn't use my brother's name to make a little money.*

We had a lot of good players on our team, a lot of talent. Our quarterback was Bernard Hall, who had played at OU, and later played in the Arena Football League when he got out. Stacy King, who played for the Chicago Bulls and Tracy Moore, who played with the Rockets, both had brothers in prison that played on our penitentiary football and basketball teams. But I was the leader.

The warden knew he wouldn't win unless I played and scored all the touchdowns on offense and played middle linebacker. He brought me up to his office and said, "The inmates are not going to go to the game unless you play."

"Well, I need some incentive," I said.

I got all my good-time days back and after the game, which we won, I won the watch for the Most Valuable Player. I won that watch for three years straight. When I'd go to the different penitentiaries to play football and basketball, there'd always be a long line of prisoners waiting just to see who I was.

"You're John Starks's brother?" they'd ask me. The players were all out there to hurt me—a lot of them were Chicago Bulls fans—because they wanted to out-do John. But they weren't going to come out there and bully me without me standing up. They didn't know that John got his toughness from me. If they wanted a piece of John, they were going to have come through me to take it. I was transferred a lot—I served time in almost every prison in Oklahoma—but whichever one I was in, when John would send me boxes and boxes of tennis shoes—I'd get seven boxes of Adidas at a time—I'd give the shoes out to all the inmates.

You can't let anyone mess with you in prison. For a long time, I got into fights constantly. People in prison are going to test you. A lot of the time, I can remember sitting in my cell thinking I wasn't going to get out alive. If someone did something to me, I knew I was capable of killing someone. Once they made the mistake of transferring Willie Hill, who killed my Auntie Anita and cousin Shelly, to the same prison that I was in. Luckily, for him, they realized what they were doing and transferred me out before he came in.

If you can't protect yourself in prison you're lost. If you can't handle yourself, they're going to take you. If you're weak, they're going to have their way with you. Many times when I saw people taking advantage of guys who couldn't defend themselves, I'd say, "Leave him alone, man. He didn't do shit to you. Leave him alone."

I had a lot to work out in prison. I had a lot of frustrations with my mother built up inside me. When I was locked up I had to deal with it myself, kind of like doing my own therapy on myself. I had to get over those feelings because they were killing me. I still have a lot of anger built up in me, a lot, over what happened when I was a kid. It doesn't take much to set me off, and I think what happened with my mother is behind that.

John sent me money, the shoes and bought me a television. He would visit me twice every year, once when he came home from New York in the summer and once before he went back in the fall, but I always felt that everybody got to reap the rewards of his career except *me. I was stuck in prison, sitting in my cell and watching whatever games I could see on television. I couldn't go to the games. Even when I made parole, I couldn't go to the games because I couldn't leave Oklahoma. It was sad. But that's life; deal with it. Going through the penitentiary system, I had to be a man.*

CHAPTER 8

LIVING THE DREAM, FACING COLD REALITY

"Work hard, be patient and take control of the situation on the floor."

—Larry Brown, Starks's first coach in the NBA
with the San Antonio Spurs

oach Hamilton had been an assistant coach at the University of Kentucky under Joe B. Hall for 12 years, but Oklahoma State was his first head coaching job. A few Division II colleges had been interested in me attending their schools, because I would have had two more years of eligibility to play. I also made a visit to Appalachian State College in North Carolina, which was a Division I school, but playing for Oklahoma State was my dream come true. It was only one hour from Tulsa by car and my grandmother came to watch every home game, as she had at Oklahoma Junior College. Even my mother, who wasn't much into basketball and had never seen me play, saw a game on television that we played against Nebraska.

Basketball in Stillwater was a big event. Henry Iba had coached there and won the first back-to-back NCAA basketball titles in 1945 and 1946. For the first time, I played before huge crowds. Coach Hamilton started me right away because he saw that I loved to play defense, I loved doing the dirty work: hustling for loose balls, setting picks, giving up my body. Coach Hamilton and I were a good match, because he needed somebody to jump-start the program, and I needed somewhere where I could show what I was capable of doing.

Coach Hamilton knew that there were a lot of good basketball players from Tulsa. He recruited Dumas and me and other Tulsa high school players. Although Tulsa is not the size of Chicago or New York, there have been several good ballplayers from here, including NBA players such as Etan Thomas, Lee Mayberry, and Ryan Humphrey.

I played in all 30 of Oklahoma State's games during the 1987-88 season, and although we only played .500 basketball, I averaged 15.4 points per game, making almost 50 percent of my field goal attempts. I also averaged nearly five rebounds and five assists per game. Larry Brown, who was the coach of our Big-12 rival, the University of Kansas, told our assistant coach Bill Self that he thought I had the potential to play in the NBA. That reinforced what Coach Trickey said to me.

But what really inspired me was the birth of my son, John Jr. that summer, and having a wife like Jackie to support me. I was only 21 years old when Jackie gave birth to our son on June 27, 1986, but I chose to be in the delivery room. I thought I was going to be one of those fathers who passed out when he saw all that, but it was a very enjoyable moment being in the delivery room with my wife while she gave birth to my son—and later with my two daughters, too. I was very fortunate. It was just a glorious moment. The pain on her face described everything. I can look back on it and say I was there for her and I experienced the joy of a new life being brought into this crazy and beautiful world.

J.J.'s birth motivated me to go out and work even harder. Before then, I was playing only for myself. I was dependent only on myself and to Monty and my mother and Callie West, to lesser degrees. I'm the type of person who doesn't need much to survive. I came from a family that didn't need much to survive.

So I really wasn't truly, truly motivated until I found out Jackie was pregnant. The birth of my son made me work even harder, because I knew I had to support my wife and my son. When I was a student, we lived mostly off of Jackie's earnings from the bank. But the driving force in my mind then became to provide for my family. I wanted to be a respectable family man. I wanted to be a good father, because I could remember wanting to have a father.

After the season, Coach Hamilton had arranged for me to go play under Paul Westphal at Grand Canyon College in Arizona, a NAIA school, where I still had college eligibility, but then Westphal got an assistant coaching job with the Phoenix Suns. Larry Brown, coming off winning the 1988 National Championship at Kansas with Danny Manning, had recently been hired as the head coach of the San Antonio Spurs. Since he liked my game, I went to Texas in the summer of 1988 so I could play in the Spurs' preseason camp. Less than two years after I'd been kicked out of Northern Oklahoma and went to work at the Safeway in Tulsa, I got an agent, Ron Grinker, and an opportunity to play in the NBA.

The summer between attending Oklahoma State and trying out for the San Antonio Spurs, I worked putting up tin roofs on buildings at the Oklahoma State branch in Tulsa, as well as Tulsa University and the Langston University campus in Tulsa. One day it was raining and I was walking on the steel beams atop a building and I slipped and fell through the fiberglass insulation. I caught myself on one of the sheet metal slabs as I was falling by hooking my forearm over it. I was just hanging there looking at how far down it was. I would've at least broken both my legs if I had fallen right through. One of my co-workers reached down and pulled me back up onto the steel beam. Then he said, "You need to get going to camp because you're going to kill yourself if you keep working here."

When I put on my first NBA jersey, I told myself that I was living my dream. I had a good summer-league camp with San Antonio in 1988. Larry Brown wanted to sign me, but the Spurs management wouldn't give me even a guarantee of $10,000 to come into their preseason camp so my agent told me to turn down their offer. Looking back on it now, I probably should have accepted San Antonio's offer and played for them. Brown is a great coach. He's the one coach I would've loved to play for. He was kind of like Pat Riley; he saw players' potential and got the best out of them.

Don Nelson was both the general manager and coach of the Warriors and I entered their rookie camp and ended up making their team. In one preseason game against the Portland Trail Blazers, I got the ball in the post and turned and dunked over Clyde Drexler, one of the great leapers in the game. In another, against the Lakers in Hawaii, I came down on a two-on-one fast-break with Magic back. I had Tellis Frank on my left-hand side, and I dished the ball to him and he made the dunk.

A minute later, I came back down on the same deal, the same exact play, and this time I said to myself, "I'm going to go over the top of Magic." So I went up to dunk on him and he reached up and caught me in midair. Magic was six foot nine and 240 pounds, a strong man. He got called for the foul and was shocked. I was shocked that I'd missed the dunk.

After the play, Nellie told me, "Go over and thank Magic because he could've ended your career right there." So I went over to Magic and thanked him.

Nelson signed me for the $100,000 minimum salary. In an 82-game season, I played in only 36 games. For most of my rookie year, my position was at the end of the bench. Nelson wasn't keen on rookies, plus I was a free agent who hadn't come in as a high draft choice so I was on the bottom of the totem pole. But when he put me in games, I played well. I was a point guard at that time and wore No. 30.

Golden State had some very good players. Winston Garland was the starting point guard and Mitch Richmond out of Kansas State, another Big-12 school, and Chris Mullin were the leading scorers. Ralph Sampson played center. I felt like I could play against anybody if I was given the opportunity, but Nelson played me less than ten minutes a game, and I scored only four points a game.

When I first made the team, Nelson wanted to sign me to a two-year contract, but I didn't want to sign for the money he was offering. We were at serious odds. Nelson has a huge ego, and I crossed the line with him by not signing that contract. From then on, he made it terrible for me by sticking me on the bench and not playing me.

He took things personally, and as a coach you can't do that because nobody's perfect. Later on, it got him in trouble with Chris Webber. He thought everyone would be on his side with Webber, but it's the players who make the game, not the coaches.

At the end of the 1988-89 season, Nelson cut me, calling me "too wild." But that was a cop-out. All the players on that Golden State team were wild. That's the kind of players Nelson likes. That's his offense, small man ball, run the ball up the court, pull up and let it fly.

One of the reasons I got such little playing time was that 25 games into the season, Nelson brought in Steve Alford, the former star at Indiana University, to play the backup point guard, my position. That's when I had it out with Nelson. He doesn't like players who stand their ground. He likes players to knuckle under and do as he says. I was a rookie who didn't have a leg to stand on, but I've always felt that if I see something that isn't right, I have to speak up. So I went into his office.

"I'm not getting enough playing time," I told him.

"You need more seasoning," Nelson said.

"But I'm playing well in practice against the guys you're playing ahead of me," I said.

"John, you've got to respect my decision," he said. "I'm the coach and you're the player."

The dual roles of general manager and coach didn't suit Nelson well. He abused his powers. Nelson is from the old school. He feels like the rookie needs to earn his dues. I thought Coach Nelson's doghouse was the worst in the league because it had one way in and no way out.

When I got to Golden State I started seeing basketball as a business. It was a rude awakening for me. I watched Terry Teagle go through hell with Don Nelson. Teagle was in the last year of his contract and Nelson wanted to pay him below value on his next contract and Teagle wouldn't accept it. He thought he should get paid more, and rightfully so, because he was having a great year.

After Terry turned down his contract offer, Nelson wouldn't play him. He sat him on the end of the bench. We would be blowing teams out by 30 points and Nelson wouldn't put him in the game. I watched Teagle go through that whole ordeal and he continued to work hard, shooting before and after practice, lifting weights, keeping himself ready no matter what. His response to an unfair situation taught me about professionalism in the game; that no matter what you go through, you've got to be prepared to play.

Mitch Richmond ended up getting hurt, and Nelson had no choice but to play Terry Teagle. It was a game against the Lakers and Teagle went off and scored over 20 points and after that game, Nelson had to play him, he couldn't sit him back down on the bench. Teagle had a great year and when contract-signing time came around, Nelson had to pay him the money anyway.

But that whole situation taught me a lot about Don Nelson as a coach and as a man. I didn't like that he would put another man through something like that. Pat Riley was both a coach and general manager with the Miami Heat, but he would never do something like not play a man over a contract dispute, because Pat was all about winning. He may not like you, but if you can help him win, he's going to play you.

Coach Riley and Anthony Mason went through their little wars with each other in New York, but when Riles got down to Miami, who was it that he brought in to help him win? Mase. Riles didn't sacrifice winning because of personal conflicts. He was a former player who understood players. He knew how to deal with people. After the Teagle situation, I realized that pro basketball was strictly a business, and that's how I approached it from then on.

Nelson cut me because he was bringing in Saruanas Marciulionis from Lithuania and Tim Hardaway from UTEP and thought I was expendable. I didn't let being cut get me down. I told myself that I wasn't even supposed to be playing in the NBA. I was supposed to have played that season at Grand Canyon College. When Nelson cut me, I told him, "Thanks for giving me the opportunity to play in the NBA" and I meant it.

When I came home to Tulsa, Darryl Madden, my old friend who I'd played with at Northern Oklahoma, said to me, "John, do you understand what you have done? Two years ago, you were in the streets playing against me, and now you just finished playing for Golden State in the NBA." I hadn't thought of it that way

It was a double whammy. The Pistons were supposedly scared away from signing me and Cedar Rapids missed out on making the playoffs. I worried that I'd blown my chance to make it back into the NBA. But I always tried to put a positive spin on things. I kept telling myself, "The League wants players who can play, and I can play." I wasn't going to give up. Overcoming hardship, I already told you, was second nature to me.

The summer of '89, before playing in the CBA, I twisted my ankle badly playing in the Pop-Off Tournament in Dallas and it wouldn't heal properly. Mel Daniels, who played for The Indiana Pacers and was a scout for the team, asked me to come to Indiana to play in their summer league. He thought I had a good chance of making the team. I went to Indiana to try out with the Pacers, but my ankle just wasn't right. I told Mel, "I just can't go." But I was close to becoming a teammate of Reggie Miller's.

Right after the CBA season, I played the following summer for the Memphis Rockers in the World Basketball League, a short-lived league that consisted of players six foot five and under. It was a kamikaze game, all fast break, helter-skelter pace up and down the floor. I made sure to stay out of trouble, and I didn't say a word to the refs.

Jackie and I started to feel the strain of raising a family and keeping a marriage intact down in Memphis. It was the third city we had lived in over a year's time. We were living in an apartment complex in Memphis, and I had just come back home from a road trip with the Rockers and was going out to the home of Andre Turner, a teammate, to shoot some pool. Jackie was upset that I was going out; just after getting in off a road trip.

Jackie didn't want me to go, so she went to the balcony and started throwing all my clothes out onto the sidewalk. I was already in my car when I saw her throwing the clothes all over the place and I just stopped, put my car in park, opened the door and ran upstairs and grabbed her. I was about to hit her when I caught myself. I really did. I had to catch myself, because I saw myself repeating what I had witnessed growing up, watching men beat up on my mother so often.

I said to myself, "No, I can't do this," and to this day, I have never hit Jackie, thank God. I had to stop the wife-beating cycle I saw my mother endure as a kid. I was taught when I was little, never to hit a girl. But seeing Jackie throw all my clothes off the balcony like that produced a knee-jerk reaction in me. I hated it when as a kid I used to see my mother throw one of her husbands or boyfriends clothes out of the house.

Jackie is a strong woman—and she saw a lot growing up, too. Sometimes she would do something like that to get a response out of me. I'm not sure why, but I rarely showed my emotions off the basketball court. On the basketball court, I had no trouble expressing what I felt, but off the court I saw it as a sign of weakness. So I held everything in. It got me in a lot of trouble sometimes, like in Game 7 in Houston, where before the game I couldn't talk to anybody, not Coach Riley or Patrick, about my frustration over Hakeem tipping my last shot of Game 6. I put too much pressure on myself. As I've gotten older, I've learned to let go, especially with Jackie.

Jackie:

When I met John I knew there was something special about him. It wasn't just love at first sight. I knew that he had the drive to go after this goal that he had set for himself. So that was very special to me, seeing the insides of someone that I was going to spend the rest of my life with. I was all for it. I wanted to be with him, to be right there beside him to go for what he wanted. It wasn't difficult because it was just part of our life real early on. Even our wedding night, I said, "Ok, this is going to be interesting."

I'm a very emotional person and I communicate quickly. I don't shut down. I let John know what I'm feeling. I do show my emotions very quickly. John probably knows that inside of me is a woman who is not going to put up with being hit. He probably wanted to hit me a lot of times, but he knows that I wouldn't tolerate it.

I knew he was a very emotional person and when I challenged him over the years it was just to get a little feedback from him because especially in the beginning, I only saw that emotion of his on the court. So I pushed him sometimes to get a little reaction from him.

CHAPTER 9

JOHN STARKS: NEW YORK KNICK

"John made himself into one of the elites of the league at the off-guard position. What he is great at is competing. He brought that energy every night. The ability to compete every time he took the floor is a talent not everybody possesses."

—Greg Anthony, a teammate on the New York Knicks

In July, I went out to Los Angeles to play in the NBA summer league at Loyola Marymount College. Dick McGuire, the Knicks' head scout had seen me play in the CBA All-Star game, and he told me that he liked my aggressiveness, toughness and athleticism. Then McGuire told the Knicks' general manager, Al Bianchi, about me.

Around the league, McGuire told me, there was still a dark cloud hanging over my head, I had attended five different colleges and played for three of them; Nelson had called me "too wild," and then I had the ref-bumping incident in the CBA. But

Bianchi told me he was going to roll the dice and give me a chance by bringing me into the Knicks' preseason camp and he gave me a $10,000 guarantee. A few years earlier, he'd signed Johnny Newman as a free agent and Johnny had just finished playing three solid seasons for the Knicks.

"I like the way you jump over people," Bianchi told me. "You're strong, you don't do everything right, but I can tell you want it. Play hard, be consistent and leave the referees alone."

I had wanted to play for the Chicago Bulls because of Michael, but I was real excited about going to New York. I was coming in with a lot of confidence. But I still didn't feel fully part of the team, and just like when I went to the San Antonio rookie camp, I came into the Knicks' preseason camp with the Knicks just looking to play well. I wanted to impress them, but I also wanted to impress the rest of the 24 other teams in the NBA at that time, too. That way if I didn't make the Knicks, another team might sign me. A minor-league player usually receives only a minimum of chances to win an NBA job, and you have to make the best of them.

When I got to New York, Stu Jackson was the coach, and I realized early on that my chances of making the team were slim. The Knicks already had veteran guards in Mark Jackson, Trent Tucker, Gerald Wilkins, along with my childhood hero, Maurice Cheeks. But they had also just signed a five-foot-seven guard, Greg Grant, to a guaranteed $300,000 contract. That seemed like a pot of gold to me after playing in the CBA.

I played well, but in the last practice before the final cut, I decided the only way I had a chance to make the team was to do something spectacular. We were playing a scrimmage and I got the ball on a breakaway with Patrick Ewing between the basket and me and I made up my mind that I was going to jump over this seven-footer and dunk the ball. I like a challenge. When you show players you can go over the top, you earn a lot of respect. I used to love watching Dr. J and David Thompson dunk over taller players. A dunk makes an instant statement. It gains respect, it intimidates. It's more than just two points.

I had received a pass at half-court and saw Patrick running up and I waited for him to get a little bit ahead of me so I could go over him. I took off on my left leg and just as I was reaching the peak of my jump and was ready to extend with my right hand for a one-handed, tomahawk jam, Patrick blocked my dunk and I fell hard to the floor.

I thought I'd torn my knee up and Patrick did, too. He was standing above me going, "You all right? You all right?" I thought my career was over. I was in agony. I let out this big roar. I'd never been hurt really bad before.

Jeff Van Gundy, the Knicks' assistant coach then, told me later that Stu and the coaches were all ready to bring me aside and tell me that I was cut. I was this CBA refugee in their eyes, and if I hadn't tried to dunk over the franchise center on the last day of practice in the final minutes of a scrimmage, I would've been toast. But instead of cutting me, the Knicks put me on their injured reserve list. It's an NBA rule that you can't cut an injured player.

When I made the team, Coach Jackson gave me a couple of days to go back to Tulsa and get my family and drive them up to New York. My wife and son had remained in Oklahoma to see if I was going to make the team or not. I had a blue Mercury Cougar and we packed up our belongings and I drove it all the way back to New York.

In Pennsylvania, we ran into this heavy blizzard and Jackie started crying, saying, "We need to pull over."

"I can't pull over," I said, "I need to get back to New York."

I got behind a semi, right on his tail and I let him know I was right behind him. If he had made any false move, there's no telling what would've happened. Once we got close to New

Jersey, the blizzard let up and I went by that semi and he blew his horn and I honked my horn and drove the rest of the way into New York.

Going over the George Washington Bridge and heading north on the Henry Hudson Parkway and onto the Bronx River Parkway, I didn't know the roads, so I was driving slowly. Suddenly, this car filled with young people cut right in front of me like they wanted to hit me and I said, "What in the world? Welcome to New York."

The season started, and the Knicks got off to a real bad start. After about 12 games, there were rumors in the papers that they were going to fire Stu and hire John McLeod, the former Phoenix Suns coach and a good friend of Bianchi's. Luckily, I hadn't torn anything in my knee and I rehabbed it and was feeling much better. The Knicks had until December 24 to cut me, or my contract would be guaranteed, which meant that I'd earn the NBA yearly minimum of $100,000 at the time. I had a wife and a kid, J.J. was three at the time, so earning that money was very important to me. My wife was still clipping coupons out of the newspapers and looking for bargains at Pathmark.

The deadline was coming up—it was like December 5— and the other players on the Knicks were telling me: "Lay low. Act like you're still hurt. If you stay on the injured list until the 24th then your money will be guaranteed for the season whether you end up getting cut or not."

But I told them, "That's not me. If I'm ready to go, I'm ready to go."

I was going to go into Stu's office the next day and tell him, "Look, I'm 100 percent. Either play me or let me go. I'm not the kind of person to just sit around."

The Knicks had an open roster spot at the time because Trent Tucker got hurt, so Stu took me off the injured reserve list and activated me on December 7, 1990, for a game against the Bulls in Chicago. I was given a uniform with the No. 3 on it.

In my first game as a Knick, I subbed in for Kiki Vandeweghe, and there I was guarding Michael Jordan. Neither Michael nor I could have possibly known that over the next six seasons we would wind up facing off against each other in 21 playoff games over four memorable Bulls-Knicks playoff series.

John McLeod had replaced Stu as coach before the Bulls game, which we lost. The team had started the season with nine losses in its first 16 games and was in the midst of losing eight out of nine games. My second game we played in Atlanta against the Hawks and Dominique Wilkins, who with Jordan, were the game's greatest leapers and dunkers. The Hawks were also one of the best teams in the league with Glen "Doc" Rivers and Spud Webb.

McLeod put me in the game early to replace Kiki again, and I played the shooting guard as Gerald Wilkins moved over to play the small forward. McLeod loved my attitude. He called me a tiger.

"Go out there and play like a tiger," he told me when he put me in the game. "Don't think, just play basketball."

It was a big Saturday night crowd, and I just started playing like I used to play at Oklahoma Junior College. In a lot of those games I used to scoop the ball off the court and take one dribble and dunk over centers. Basketball is basketball. It doesn't matter whom you're going up against. If you start worrying about your opponents, you've already lost the battle. McLeod kept me in the game the rest of the way.

In a losing cause, I played 33 minutes, scored 20 points, grabbed six rebounds, dished out four assists and had two steals. I was flying all over the place. I was playing the pick-and-roll game with Patrick just like I had with Richard Dumas at Oklahoma State. I hadn't realized how good an outside shooter Patrick was until that game. I'd run out on the break and get an outlet pass from Charles Oakley and either go right to the basket or look for Patrick. Oakley was a great teammate, because I knew if anything went down, Charles would be there to get my back. He did everything with aggressiveness, and I liked that in a power forward.

After that Hawks game, I heard McLeod telling reporters: "Starks deserves playing time. He deserves as much as we can give him." I was really starting to feel like I belonged.

Three nights later, I stepped onto the Madison Square Garden floor for the first time to play in a regular-season game. I was ready and I expected to play well. I knew I had to step up and show that I could perform in pressure situations. Coach McLeod put me in halfway through the first quarter and right away I drilled three three-pointers. The Garden crowd, which was quiet until then and had booed us at the start of the game, lit up. I heard some fans yell, "Way to go, Number 3." Most of them couldn't read my name on the back of my jersey and had never seen or heard of John Starks before.

At one point in that game against the Miami Heat, we scored 20 consecutive points and we blew them out. I knew Coach McLeod expected me to give the team a spark coming off the bench and that's what I did. My teammates seemed to feed off my enthusiasm. One play in particular sticks out in my mind. Patrick skied high over the rim for a rebound and passed it out to me on the wing and I took off leading the fast break. Dribbling full steam up court, I saw Patrick out of the corner of my eye streaking up behind me and I turned and dropped him a pass. Patrick went down the lane and jumped right over Heat center Rony Seikaly and jammed it in hard. I had never played with any big man before who could finish a play like that.

Over 27 minutes, I scored a career-high 22 points, making seven of 12 shots. After the game, Jackie and I went out on the town, ate a nice meal and just enjoyed New York City. I didn't even go home right away to watch the game tape. I was on Cloud Nine and didn't feel like coming down anytime soon.

Later on in the season, in a game against the Nets, I replaced Wilkins in the starting lineup because he had a bad ankle, and I scored 25 points. In the second-to-last game of the season against the Indiana Pacers, in only my second time facing Reggie Miller, coming off the bench I scored 20 points in 24 minutes, hitting on eight of nine field goal attempts and four of five three-point shots.

I was playing on the same team as Maurice Cheeks, one of my boyhood idols, but I never told him that. Mo was funny. He used to skip out on practice a lot. Older guys never like to practice, and Mo was 34 years old and in his third to last year in the league. He'd come in and do his stretching and then run up and down the floor a couple of times and say to me, "Young fellow, come out and get me." Then he'd go put some ice on his knees and stay on the sidelines for the rest of the practice. It used to crack me up.

I saw the business side of the profession again when the trading deadline came up in February and Al Bianchi tried to get Mark Jackson to renounce his contract. It would've made Mark easier to trade and Mark wouldn't do it. One day both Bianchi and McLeod cornered him at our practice court up at Purchase College in Westchester County, New York and they tried to tag-team Mark into giving into their demands.

"What do you two think?" Mark shouted. "You think you're some kind of gangsters trying to strong arm me? You aren't going to gangster me into nothing." I just watched it all while shooting free throws and I was cracking up. By then I knew the NBA low down: If you play hard and produce, you'll stay. If you don't, you move on.

Bianchi suspended Mark for insubordination and after that McLeod stopped playing him. In late February and March, we went on a 10-1 winning streak that enabled us to make the play-offs. I was playing aggressively and making some big shots, and I started playing ahead of the veteran, Trent Tucker. To Trent's credit, he was a great guy and he helped me out a great deal. He talked to me about shooting technique and how to come off picks to get a shot and about playing defense. I was new to the league and the team, and he could've been salty that I was playing in front of him, but that wasn't the case.

Mo Cheeks had replaced Mark as the starting point guard. Sometimes the Garden crowd would chant, "We want Mark." Mark had been Rookie of the Year in 1988 and an All-Star in 1989 and he was from New York, so the fans wanted to see him play. I understood that and so did Mo. There were no hard feelings between any of us. Mark and Trent knew that it was the coach's decision on who plays, and I went out there and played hard when McLeod called on me.

In 1990-91, I played in 61 games for the Knicks, almost double the amount I had played in with Golden State Warriors two years earlier, and I averaged 7.6 points, again almost double what I'd averaged with the Warriors. The Knicks finished with a 39-43 record, and in the first round of the playoffs, the Bulls swept us in three games and later went on to knock off the Lakers in five games to win their first NBA Championship. I didn't play in Games 1 or 3 of the series, but I got in for 18 minutes in Game 2 and scored six points.

CHAPTER 10

DRUGS, GUNS AND VIOLENCE

"You can take the kid out of the 'hood, but you can't take the 'hood out of the kid."

—John Starks

When I got back to Tulsa that summer, I got tested on the playgrounds. Everyone wanted to see how good I was. It is the park player's dream to challenge an NBA player, and they took it to me hard. They wanted to measure themselves against me, and that's the way it's supposed to be. I was at the next level, and that's where they were all trying to get. They wanted to see what I had. I'd watch the eyes of the kids I was going up against and they were all excited to be playing against John Starks. I felt really proud about that, and I didn't hold back, I showed them everything I had.

My youngest brother, Ju Ju, was getting into a lot of trouble around that time. He had a bad cocaine addiction, and he started running with a gang, the Pea Stones from Los Angeles. Ju Ju had hooked up with them when the family moved out to Sacramento when I started college. He got shot in his bad foot and had his cheek cut open five inches across with a knife. He was selling drugs in the Morningstar apartment complex when a guy came up behind him with a doctor's scalpel and cut open the whole right side of his face and he needed 42 stitches just to close it up.

Right around the time I played my first game for the Knicks, Ju Ju was caught selling cocaine at the Morningstar Apartments and he was sent to prison for five months. It was his first offense, and at 18 years old, it was his first time behind bars, but the experience didn't teach him anything. He went right back to shooting, robbing and selling dope. I tried to work with him to get him off drugs. I knew he was a good kid, but he had a knack for getting into trouble. I would go to his apartment with a Bible and tell him to get down on the floor and pray. We used to read the Word together, but he just wasn't ready at the time to receive it.

People in the neighborhood would tell me, "You've got to get your little brother off the streets. How come you're making all that money with the Knicks and you can't help him out?" I tried to get him into the best treatment money would buy, but there was only so much that I could do. After a while I saw that I could only leave it in God's hands and that's what I did. But I prayed that I wouldn't wake up one morning and get a call saying that my little brother had been killed.

I went to visit Monty that summer in prison. It was hard seeing him locked up like that. It made me very sad, especially since he couldn't fully enjoy watching me play for the Knicks. I knew he would've loved to come to the Garden and hear the New York fans and yell right along with them. I tried to time my visits, especially when I got more famous, so that I wouldn't draw attention. I was worried that prison would harden Monty's heart the way it does some people. Monty always had a good heart. He'd do anything for anybody. I also wished he was out of prison so he could help me with the family.

Drugs were killing my family. My Uncle Lawrence, my mother's oldest brother, was also a drug addict. Lawrence had played football with Thomas "Hollywood" Henderson at Lexington University in Gutherie, Oklahoma, an all-black college. He got turned onto heroin then and could never kick the habit. It really upset my grandmother. Lawrence would do all right for a while, but then he'd mess up again and she'd always bring him back in because he was her son.

I would tell her all the time, "Granny, you've got to let him go. He's stressing you out."

She would look at me and say, "Son, you just don't understand. You'll never understand."

I understood she had this tremendous bond with her first son and that she wanted to see him become successful, but he never turned out that way. My grandmother always brought Lawrence back in. He always knew he had a home. She could never cut him loose and let him mess up and try to make it on his own. In a way, I was thankful that she was like that, because she'd saved my family more times than I could remember when I was young.

Now I'm pretty sure guys on the Knicks had guns for safety reasons. I had one when I played in New York and lived in Westchester and Fairfield Counties. I didn't take it in my car and ride with it or anything like that, but I did keep a gun. I grew up in circumstances where you needed a gun. It's like they say, "You can take the kid out of the 'hood, but you can't take the 'hood out of the kid." You go back to your roots. Guns were part of my life growing up, so I used to own one.

It just so happened that one summer day after my first season with the Knicks, I did have my gun in my car. I had gone to church with Jackie and J.J. and I went over to my grandmother's house after church to check in on her. I saw Lawrence lying down on the couch in my grandmother's house. I was tired of seeing the pain he was causing my grandmother because I loved her with all my heart. He was destroying both himself and her.

I told him to come outside the house, that I wanted a word with him. When he came out onto the front lawn, I said, "Man, why don't you go out and get yourself a job and do something?" Lawrence started talking crazy and then he went back inside the house and said he was going to get a knife. I walked back to my car and I got my gun from underneath the seat and held it behind my back. If Lawrence had come back out of my grandmother's house with a knife in his hand, there's no telling what I would have done.

He didn't care what he was doing to my grandmother. People like him do not care when they're an addict. It's like the movie, *Jungle Fever*, the part that Samuel L. Jackson played. Lawrence was like that. No matter what Samuel Jackson did in that movie, his mother would always bring him back in. I guess that's what my grandmother meant when she talked about the love you feel for your child. Lawrence is in his fifties now and he is still addicted to drugs, but he's locked up now. Hopefully this stint will help him get his life under control. I pray for that every night.

Ron Grinker, my agent at the time, organized a summer program in the gym at Xavier College in Cincinnati, and I went and worked out there with players like Derek Smith, Tyrone Hill, Dirk Minnifield and Brian Grant. Derek had already played nine seasons in the NBA for a number of teams and he told me, "John, you've got all the skills they can't teach. You've got a beautiful gait, you run like a thoroughbred, you've got an explosive first step, you're a leaper and you play to win. Now you've got to take it to the next level."

I went next to the Knicks' preseason camp held at the Kutscher's Hotel in the Catskills Mountains in upstate, New York. I met Anthony Mason there. He had been signed in the off season as a free agent by the Knicks after playing a total of 24 NBA games the past two seasons with the Nets and the Nuggets. I knew of Mason back when he'd been a star in the CBA playing for the Tulsa Fastbreakers. Mase used to be the man in Tulsa and he'd be the first person to tell you. He liked Tulsa. Mase was originally from Queens, but he'd come back down to Tulsa in the summer time even when the CBA season was over. Tulsa has a way of charming people. A lot of inner-city kids like Mase who come to play ball at Oral Roberts and TU, Tulsa University, end up staying here because they see how nice it is and how friendly the people are. They get here and say, "Why go back home?"

Mase got his nickname, "The Beast," in Tulsa. He used to kill people. He averaged 29.9 points a game for Tulsa one year. At 6-8, 260 pounds, Mase was the most physically intimidating player I ever played with besides Oak, Charles Oakley. But Mase could also handle the ball. He showed me how to control my own dribble better by pounding the ball and getting it more on my fingertips. Mase was a wide body while Oak was really cut and chiseled at 6-9, 245. I was like 6-2 and 180, and I tried not to run into those behemoths. But Mase and I clicked right away. We both came from similar, tough backgrounds and had to work our way up through the minor leagues, and we liked to play with a reckless abandon. When either of us would dive out of bounds for a loose ball or knock down a big shot, it spurred both of us on.

We were like brothers. Just by shooting each other a look, we both knew how to get each other up and how to calm each other down. It was good to have that kind of bond with a teammate, because when Pat Riley became the coach of the New York Knicks that summer, signing a four-year contract, Mase and I both knew we were moving up to the big time.

CHAPTER 11

RILEY'S SON

"He's one of the great competitors I have been around in my life and I love him dearly for that competitive nature of his."

—Pat Riley on John Starks

I had already played for some intense coaches in college and the pros. Ken Trickey, Don Nelson and John McLeod all yelled a lot, but Pat Riley had a different intensity. He was like a war general, always going over his notes before a practice or a game, fully prepared for every contingency that could happen out on the court. Even the way he dressed with his Armani suits and his hair slicked back; Riles paid attention to detail.

Coach Riley was a great teacher about life and the game. Basketball is like the game of life in some ways, because a player has to deal with a lot of the same stuff on the basketball court that he does in life. Coach Riley taught us how to be professionals. If a young player coming into this league doesn't know how to be a professional, he's not going to last long. You can't come into the league and act the fool.

Coach Riley taught us what it meant to be a professional by teaching us how to approach the game, to never be late for a practice or a game, and how to conduct ourselves on and off the court. He was a big believer that what you do off the court affects what you do on the court. Riles taught us that if everything is stable in your life off the court, it's easier to walk on the court and focus on the game. He took care of everything for the team, because he wanted his players thinking about basketball. Riles knew right away when one of us was affected by something going on in our lives off the court.

The very first day of practice, Coach Riley preached defense. "Offense is going to be up and down," he said, "but defensive intensity has to stay consistently high. Defense keeps you in games." He figured we weren't an explosive offensive team—which we weren't—so he built the team around defense.

Defense, defense, we practiced it so much it just became a habit. Riles thought I could be a very good defensive player, and he kept at me all the time over it. He'd tell me, "Nobody in this league can go from point A to B to C as quickly as you, but you've got to do it on every defensive stop."

Riley was a young coach, only 46 years old at the start of the 1991-92 season, but he had already won four NBA championships, one as a player with the Lakers and three as their head coach. He was coming home in a way, coaching the Knicks, because before he went to the University of Kentucky to play basketball under legendary coach Adolph Rupp, he had grown up in upstate New York. And Riles was tough; his father had been a minor-league catcher and his brother, an NFL defensive back. Riles himself was a draft pick of the Dallas Cowboys and he hadn't even played football in college.

In Los Angeles, Riles had Magic, Kareem, James Worthy, Byron Scott and Michael Cooper so he ran the "Showtime" fast-break offense. In New York he knew we had a different group of players. We had some players who could get out and run like Mark Jackson, Gerald Wilkins, Mase, Greg Anthony, and me, but for the most part we were a half-court, grind-'em-down team. Riles started building that style of play right from the first day of practice.

Xavier McDaniel, "X," had come over in a trade with the Phoenix Suns for Trent Tucker and Jerrod Mustaf, and Anthony had been the Knicks' first-round draft pick. Anthony had won a national championship with UNLV in college, and he was tough and fiery. Our practices were just like wars.

Oakley and X had a history. They had gotten into a big fight that had escalated into the stands the previous year when the Knicks played Phoenix. Right from the first day, they just went at it in practice like two bucking broncos. They would just lock each other up underneath the basket and grab each other. They were battling, battling, battling, and usually Riles didn't do a thing to stop them. Finally, Oak and X would stare each other down, but after a while they realized that they were teammates now and after that it was cool.

Oak and Mase were the same way. Mase was just coming in trying to prove that he belonged, and Oak was well established, but neither one of them was giving ground. All I heard that first day of practice was the sound of bodies crashing, "crash, pow, pow, pow," the slapping of skin. I said to myself, "Man, I'm not going to the basket today. I'm not going to go in there today."

With Ewing, 7-0, 255; X, 6-7 218; Mase, Oakley and also James Donaldson, 7-2, 278; I didn't want to go into the lane too much and get into that mix. I was 6-2, 180 at the time; I didn't start building up my body fully until after I hurt my knee in the 1993-94 season. But that first team under Riley was one physical team, and nobody in the league that year liked playing us much.

Riles had a lot to do with my growth as a player. I went from being a no-name player to being one of the best shooting guards in the NBA under his tutelage. I'd always worked hard on my own game, but I needed coaches at every level to enhance my play. Instead of constantly reprimanding me when I took bad shots or made turnovers, Riles let me have a freer rein. He told me that I had a lot of skills and he was going to give me freer license on the court so that my talent could flourish. The players started calling me "Riley's Son" and kidded me by saying, "Who's your daddy, Riles?"

That's just the type of team we were. We all needled each other a lot. We all thought alike. Every 'hood, every black community, is pretty much the same, and we were all from the inner city, all different cities, Mark and Mase from New York, Patrick from Boston, Oak from Cleveland, Greg Anthony from Las Vegas and me from Tulsa. We'd all done things growing up that we shouldn't have gotten involved with. None of us were choirboys.

We would say things to each other that reporters listening in and not knowing our backgrounds and rapport with each other would take the wrong way. Riles liked us to get on each other, because then he didn't have to do it so much himself. For example, we always used to kid Oak because he couldn't jump so well and he had a problem dunking the ball and finishing around the basket. Oak would razz me for talking too much.

Oak would say to me, "You've got a big mouth," and Mark would say, "You can't shut John up. He's always talking too much." Oak called "Dougie" (Gerald Wilkins), me and "G" (Greg Anthony), the "three riff-raff." He'd say, "You all talk too much. Like Scottie Pippen, he talked too much, too. I had to put up with Scottie, and now I got to put up with you three."

As a team, we thrived on the infighting, and the city seemed to feed off our energy just like we fed off the city's energy. We had a New York, blue-collar, in-your-face attitude. We took on the personality of the city we played in. When I head-butted Reggie Miller in the 1993 playoffs, Patrick and Oak shoved me in the chest and dressed me down for doing it, but the next day we all got over it and went back to the business of beating the Pacers.

When Mase got into trouble with Coach Riley, he always came back and played harder and better. I always knew how to talk to Mase and bring him back to his senses. Mase is Mase. Mase is going to do what Mase is going to do. I'd run into a lot of people like Mase growing up in Tulsa. You had to let him go on his temper tantrums and then when he calmed down, you talked sense to him.

Some adversity on a team can be a good thing, just like with the current Lakers team. Pat Riley, just like Phil Jackson, knew how to use the discord to make us play harder and wiser. I usually played better when I was angry. The more my heart pounded, the more intense the atmosphere, the better I played. I've never had a problem of focusing when the heat's turned up.

Certain coaches know how to read certain guys. They know what makes them tick and how to motivate them to play their best, and Riles was that kind of coach for me. Kobe Bryant experienced that same growth as a player when Phil Jackson became the Lakers coach. Kobe was a very solid player until then, but he didn't become a great player until Jackson put his faith in him.

Coach Riley would tell me, "John, you're one of those guys who feels he's got to smack someone who gets in your face. You're whole career you've been told, 'No, you can't do it,' and that's created a defiant, combative competitiveness in you that I like."

I didn't think about it that way, but I knew what he meant. I thought a lot about how I come up through the CBA and knowing where I came from and how I had to travel the difficult road to the NBA made me appreciate the life that much more. Playing in the CBA made me work that much harder because I knew there were players out there working to take my place, just like I took somebody's place.

Greg Anthony would say to me, "John, you've earned Coach Riley's trust. You and him have a special relationship. You project this tremendous faith in your ability and Riles never waivers in his belief that you can reach another level."

My minutes under Riley were up almost double from the year before, and instead of me looking to set up my teammates, they were starting to look to set me up. Two years after Nelson had cut me from the Warriors, I was the Knicks' second-leading scorer, averaging 13.9 points per game on a team that was on its way to winning 51 games and tying the Boston Celtics for first place in the Atlantic Division. I shot 45 percent from the field, the highest ever in my career, and almost 35 percent from beyond the three-point arc.

I was still coming off the bench, but I didn't mind, because I was playing starter's minutes. After a game against the Nets in December where I scored 27 points, Coach Riley told me, "Maybe I shouldn't be saying this to you, but the way we rate players, you're coming off as the most productive off-guard in the Atlantic Division."

Riles would warn me about dribbling or shooting too much to the point where Patrick would come out of the post looking for the ball. The ball had to go inside-out in Riley's offense, meaning Riles wanted Patrick to get the ball in the post first and then he had to kick it out if he didn't have anything. Riles wanted us to attack the basket. That's how championships are won over the years. I haven't seen a jump-shooting team win a championship yet.

If I got distracted on the court and started trash-talking, Riles would pull me out of the game and tell me, "Less talking, more playing." If I pounded my chest and shouted to the rafters after some plays, he'd pull me aside and tell me, "Play big and shrink. Be humble." Generally, Riles let me play my game. Bianchi said he put me on the stage, but it was Riley who gave me the part.

Coach reined me in when he felt I crossed the line between playing team ball and too much individual play, but he knew my game was about being aggressive both on the offensive and defensive ends. If a coach yells at you after every shot you miss or continually questions your decisions out on the court, then it's impossible to make something happen, and my job was to bring that spark to the team. Some of the players might have thought Riles treated me with kid gloves or praised me too much, but they fed off the energy I brought onto the court. It lifted them up. They saw how hard I played, and that made them all play harder.

In two games against the Warriors in late January and early February, I scored a combined 39 points. I played with even more energy and emotion against the Warriors, because I wanted to show the whole organization, but particularly Don Nelson, that he had made a mistake in letting me go.

In an overtime win against Phoenix in February, Riles put me on the Suns' All-Star guard, Kevin Johnson, with 8:30 minutes remaining in the game and the Knicks trailing 83-80. From that point on, Johnson hit just two of six shots, turned over the ball twice and slipped while trying to make a play that could have won it for the Suns near the end of regulation. I scored 12 points on four-for-seven shooting.

After the game, the Suns' coach, Cotton Fitzsimmons said, "I told my guys, all the other guys on the Knicks have their money. Starks is just out there trying to make it."

Kevin Johnson said, "What impressed me the most tonight is how strong Starks takes it to the basket—and even more importantly, left-handed. When he played with Golden State, he couldn't dribble left-handed and go to the basket at all. That shows me that the guy's been working on his game—I mean really working on his game."

Over the last ten games of the regular season, I scored 28 points against Chicago on eight-for-15 shooting from three-point land, 21 points against Cleveland and 28 points against Milwaukee on five-for-eight, three-point shooting. I'm not mentioning my big scoring games to boast. I'm trying to show how far I'd come from when I played for the Warriors and I barely made it off the bench. I hit on 94 three-point shots in the 1991-92 season, compared to 27 the previous year, and my three-point shooting percentage jumped from 29 percent to nearly 35 percent.

There is a prejudice in this league against playing guys who aren't high draft picks and who play with the abandon that I did. It took coaches like John McLeod and Pat Riley to recognize that I was a winning basketball player and to give me a chance to play. It also helped that the star of the team, Patrick Ewing, respected me and the way I played. He liked that I came out every night ready to compete and that I was tough.

The NBA is a star league, and New York is a superstar city. Patrick was the main man, the focal point, and he had a lot of pressure on him. Patrick and I, over time, grew to be very close, like brothers, and he really helped me. Patrick really didn't say that much. He's the type of leader who leads by example. The only thing he'd tell me sometimes is, "Slow down."

Patrick didn't like guys who didn't play hard. He expected his teammates to play as hard as he did. Once he saw my ability and that I didn't back down from anyone on the court, Patrick knew that I had his back. He's the type of person who has to trust you before he opens up to you, but once he did, he supported me like no other teammate.

People say that the Knicks' rise in the '90s corresponded with my blossoming as a player, and I like to think my energy and heart was contagious, but I also know we had a lot of players instilled with those characteristics. We fed off what we were, and we were physical and emotional. We fed off each other. We were all defensive players and a lot of us started at the same time. It was an awesome time and an awesome environment.

In 1991-92, I played in all 82 regular-season games as did Oak, Mase, X, G and Dougie. Mark Jackson and Patrick played in 81 games. The 51 games we won marked only the third time since the Knicks' last championship season in 1972-73 that a Knicks team had won more than 50 games in a regular season.

In the first round of the playoffs, we beat the Detroit Pistons in five games. The Pistons had the same nucleus of players that won them back-to-back NBA championships only two years earlier: Isiah Thomas, Joe Dumars, Mark Aguirre, Dennis Rodman and Bill Laimbeer. Dumars was the toughest defender I ever played against. He was a great shooter and a strong defender.

In the Eastern Conference Semis we faced the Bulls again. The Bulls had won 67 games in the regular season and swept Miami in the first round of the playoffs in three games. In Game 1 of the series, in Chicago, we knocked the Bulls off 94-89. I scored 12 points in 24 minutes of play. It was the Bulls' first play-off loss since Game 1 of the 1991 Finals when the Lakers beat them. Since then they had won seven straight playoff games.

With the score tied at 16 in the first quarter, I scored eight points and we went on an 11-0 run, and I hit for eight points during that stretch. Whenever Jordan wandered off me defensively, I made the Bulls pay. But I picked up my third foul early in the second quarter and Riley pulled me out of the game.

I was called for a borderline foul against Jordan with less than a minute to play, and he tied the game at 87 with two free throws, but then Patrick hit a jumper for two of his 34 points and Pippen missed a jumper with 15 seconds left and we held on for the win.

After the game, Riles said, "We came here to win, we didn't come here to play." Phil Jackson said the Bulls' six-day layoff was the reason they played so sluggishly, but Michael called it an excuse and said that we outplayed them. "Anyone who doubted the Knicks," he said, "found out they are for real and a team to be dealt with."

The Bulls came back and won Games 2 and 3, but in Game 4, we out-muscled the Bulls on the boards, pulling down 52 rebounds to their 33, and we evened the series at two games apiece. Jackson was ejected when he argued a no-call on Scottie when he drove to the basket and was knocked down by X. After the game, Phil said, "They're shoving our dribblers with two hands and that's against the rules. That's football. I think the league has to take a serious look at this type of play. You could have called a foul on every play."

X said, "They're doing the same thing to us. We're not doing as much complaining as they are."

The Bulls clearly didn't like playing physical basketball. Jim Cleamons, their assistant coach said, "It wasn't a basketball game. It was a mugging. But then the whole series has been that way." Scott Williams, their 6-10, 245-pound backup center said, "It was the roughest basketball I've ever experienced. It was forearms, hips, hands in the back; anything for position in the lane. It was like they say in wrestling—no holds barred. But if these are the rules according to the referees now, then we've got to learn to play by them."

Mark, Greg and I were diving for loose balls like Pete Rose. Patrick only scored 15 points, so Riles used a lineup of X, G, Dougie, Mase and I and we were very effective. We knew the game was turning our way when Michael missed a breakaway slam-dunk with the ball bouncing off the back of the rim all the way out to mid-court. With Patrick out of the game, we all knew we had to step it up. I scored 16 points in 25 minutes. Coach said afterward, "It took 48 minutes of unbelievable effort."

We lost Game 5 back in Chicago, and before Game 6 at the Garden, Riley told us in the locker room, "Don't let Jordan and Pippen get into the lane. That's their whole game, Michael and Scotty penetrating, breaking us down, dunking or dishing off to their big men for easy baskets."

We came out fired up and the Garden crowd was fired up. We didn't like the Bulls because they were the world champions. We tried to intimidate them by getting up in their faces, getting inside their heads so they'd start thinking about us and not the game. X really intimidated Pippen and the crowd sensed what we were trying to do. They became our sixth man just like in the championship years.

We blew the Bulls out in Game 6, 100-86. I scored a career playoff-high 27 points and held Michael to three points in the fourth quarter and 21 overall. After the game he told reporters, "Anything anyone says about us not getting it done is disrespecting the Knicks. We haven't sunk to their level. They've raised themselves to ours."

With 19 seconds left in the third quarter, Pippen intercepted a Greg Anthony pass at mid-court and took off for the basket. I chased him down and tried to come across his body and swipe the ball away. But Pippen moved the ball at the last second and instead of my hand knocking the ball away, my forearm hit Pippen's neck. His body went one way and his head went the other. I was just trying to stop him from making a lay up. It was a hard, aggressive foul and the referees called it a flagrant.

Phil Jackson said I purposefully clothes-lined Scottie and that it showed how "desperate" a player I was, but I wasn't buying it. Phil is a great coach and he's very psychologically smart; he knows about the mental part of the game and the art of war, but I just made a common basketball play, trying to come across a guy's body to swipe the ball away. If Pippen hadn't double-clutched I would've hit the ball and not gotten his neck.

I wouldn't say Scottie was a soft player. He wasn't going to hit you in the face or play physical. He was a finesse player. He used his quickness, but he'd throw an elbow or two. I had more trouble trying to score against Pippen than I did Jordan. Pippen was taller, longer, harder to get around. He made me rush my shots more because he would bother jump shots of mine that I didn't think he'd be able to get near. Pippen was a heck of a competitor, and playing with Michael brought out everything he had. If Michael sensed that one of his teammates wasn't competing, he'd bring it out of you. He'd make you compete by his example and his glare.

But besides Jordan and Grant, the Bulls weren't a physical team. Even when they got Rodman later, they were still a finesse team, because Dennis knew how to use his body to get rebounds, but I wouldn't call him a physical player. I'm sure Scottie was real happy when the Knicks decided not to re-sign X after the season, because X got right in Scottie's face and Scottie didn't like that. But there were no hard feelings between Scottie and me. He even came one summer to Tulsa to play in my charity All-Star game.

In Game 7, back in Chicago, the Bulls blew us out, 110-81. Michael was on fire, scoring 42 points and after the game he said, "This series might give us the hunger that we had last year." I scored 18 points in 30 minutes, but I was upset that we didn't give a better showing. Patrick had hurt his ankle in the fourth quarter of Game 6 and he wasn't at his intimidating best.

"It's tough," I said after the game. "All we can do now is work harder all summer to get a little better."

In the off season, Coach Riley asked me to work on my pull-up jump shot and to bulk up some because playing the two-guard position I was going up against guys like Jordan, who was 6-6, 215, Glen Rice, 6-8, 220, Drazen Petrovic, 6-5, 200 and Mitch Richmond, 6-5, 215. These guards outweighed me by 15-20 pounds and were all at least three inches taller than me. I threw my body around a lot when I played. I got my nose stuck on the ball a lot, and that's why I got knocked around so much. So I knew I had to get bigger, but it was a Catch-22, because I didn't want to lose my quickness by getting too bulked up.

Riley was very clear that he wanted us to do a lot of weightlifting. During the season, we lifted weights after every practice. But I also ate five meals a day during the summer of 1992 to get up to 190 pounds. Jeff Van Gundy came out to Tulsa that summer to work with me on my jumper to make sure I was shooting it off my fingertips and not my palm. I used to wear the "Hot Hand" gloves that kept the ball out of my palms and in my fingertips.

Coach also wanted me to improve on my overall control of my emotions on the court without sacrificing any of my intensity. He told me I had to stay in the game mentally regardless of what happened.

"I don't care if you miss three shots in a row," he said, "the official gives you a bad call, the opposing player taunts you; you have to stay in the game mentally. It's just maturing as a player."

Coaches had been telling me that ever since I started playing basketball, because I am a very emotional person. I got down on myself sometimes when I didn't play well. I did that to try to motivate myself. Sometimes that hampered me because I would get so far down it took me out of the game. I just had to learn to control my emotions better, stay focused and not let things bother me.

While working out in the training camp in Cincinnati that summer, Derek Smith told me, "You've got to take it to the next level now. Fifteen points a game and all those accolades are nowhere near enough now. Last year you were in the middle of the pack in this training camp. This year you are the star. You're putting up some good numbers in New York. Now you've got to move mountains."

"I always said a big dunk is worth more than two points. This dunk seals Game 2 of the 1993 playoffs against the Bulls. But in New York basketball circles, it's known emphatically as "The Dunk." *Nathaniel S. Butler/NBAE/Getty Images*

My grandmother is flanked by my mother on her right and Auntie Betty on her left. My mother was five and Betty four. They lived in California at the time. *Courtesy of John Starks*

My uncle, Curtis West, at Northeastern University in Tallequa, Oklahoma, thought he was sharp like Craig Sager. *Courtesy of John Starks*

My grandfather, Harold Starks, is flanked by his two daughters, Auntie Betty on the left, and my mother, Irene Starks, on the right. *Courtesy of John Starks*

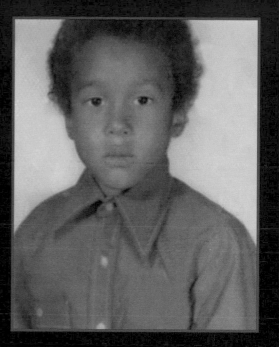

Here I am, looking serious at four years old.
Courtesy of John Starks

JuJu (left) and "Bucky" Lynn, in the kitchen on Christmas Day. JuJu is 7 and Bucky 9. JuJu's ticked off because he didn't get a new coat like Bucky did. *Courtesy of John Starks*

On the couch, from left, are Bucky, my mother, Nikki and me. JuJu and Anita are kneeling in front in our living room in the house on Elwood Street. I'm wearing my high-top Converse All-Stars, the shoes Dr. J wore, and sporting a big Afro like the doctor.
Courtesy of John Starks

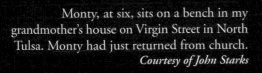

Monty, at six, sits on a bench in my grandmother's house on Virgin Street in North Tulsa. Monty had just returned from church.
Courtesy of John Starks

My mother, with her ex-husband, Kenneth Patterson, liked to smile. She was a pleasant woman.
Courtesy of John Starks

Here, I'm a senior at Tulsa Central High School. I stood 5'10" and weighed 150 pounds. As a junior I played on the junior varsity team, and I only played two games of varsity ball as a senior before I quit over a fight I had with the coach. *Courtesy of John Starks*

Jackie and I are celebrating on our wedding night, holding court at the reception at Jackie's uncle's house in Tulsa. Less than an hour later, Jackie and I were on the road, making a trip to Independence, Kansas, so I could play in a game for Oklahoma Junior College. *Courtesy of John Starks*

Monty and his first wife, Marcia, relax at a club in Tulsa after Monty had left college at Northeastern University. *Courtesy of John Starks*

Callie West is dressed in her finest and carrying her Bible as she comes out of the Greater Union Church in Tulsa.
Courtesy of John Starks

Seated around the table, from left, are JuJu, at 19, with our cousin, Antonio—my best friend growing up—and my grandmother at a restaurant in Tulsa. *Courtesy of John Starks*

My first year with the Knicks, 1990, I earned respect by dunking over the Big Chief, Robert Parish. Dunking makes a statement, especially when you're doing it over a seven-footer. Ed Pinckney (No. 54 Celtics) looks on. Pinckney was my assistant coach with the Westchester Wildfire. *Louis Capozzola/NBAE/Getty Images*

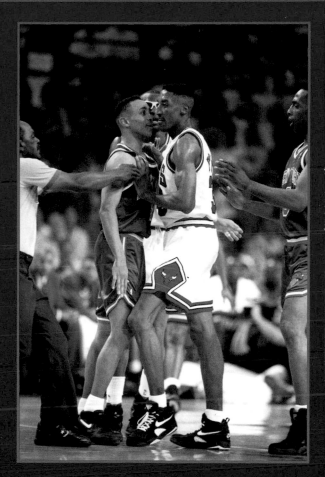

Scottie Pippen and I exchange words during the 1993 Eastern Conference Finals. In the 1992 playoffs against the Bulls, I had accidentally clotheslined Scottie as he drove to the basket. Here I'm just letting him know that I didn't appreciate something he did. Scottie would walk up on me from time to time. Horace Grant, Tony Campbell and the referee come in to break us up.
Jonathan Daniel/NBAE/Getty Images

This is the hug that Don Nelson took personally and the beginning of the end of my troubles with Nelson. It was Coach Riley's first time back in Madison Square Garden after he left the Knicks to coach the Heat. Derek Harper looks on. *AP/WWP*

I'm going up against Michael in Chicago after his return from his first retirement. Michael's wearing No. 45, and he lit me up for 55 points in his first game back at Madison Square Garden earlier in 1995. Look at Michael's perfect shooting form.
Nathaniel S. Butler/NBAE/Getty Images

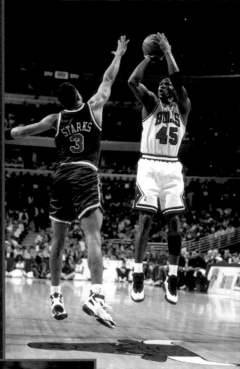

I'm playing pick-and-roll with Patrick against the Rockets. Vernon Maxwell got picked off and Hakeem Olajuwon is moving his feet to cut me off. It was a similar play at the end of Game 6 where my three-point shot to win the game and the championship was tipped by Hakeem.
NBAE/Getty Images

When we wore black sneakers, it meant that the playoffs were on. I'm going left around P.J. Brown of the Miami Heat in our controversial loss to the Heat in the 1997 playoffs. *Andy Lyons/NBAE/Getty Images*

Here I am taking the heat from a hot and steamy Jeff Van Gundy. I'm trying not to listen by focusing on the court. The "DS" on my sweatband was my tribute to my friend and former NBA player, Derek Smith, who died from an allergic reaction to a motion sickness pill he took while on a vacation cruise ship. *AP/WWP*

JOHN STARKS *MY LIFE*

My last playoff series with the Knicks was in 1998. Losing to the Pacers was always hard to swallow. I had no idea that the following season I'd no longer be a Knick. *AP/WWP*

In the Houston Summit after a Finals game in 1994, from left, are my oldest brother, Tony, my mother, my sister, Anita, my mother's ex-husband, Kenneth, and my sister's husband, Reuben. The woman in front I don't know. *Courtesy of John Starks*

It was bittersweet returning to watch the Knicks make it back to the NBA Finals in 1999. I would rather have been on the court, but sitting on Celebrity Row next to Spike, while it was strange, wasn't too bad either. *AP/WWP*

I got traded back to the Golden State Warriors in 1999 and Latrell Sprewell came to the Knicks. It was weird being a Warrior again after I started my career there 11 years earlier. I switched to the No. 9 because Vonteego Cummings, whom I've coached for the last two years with the Westchester Wildfire in the USBL, wore the No. 3.
Jed Jacobsohn/NBAE/Getty Images

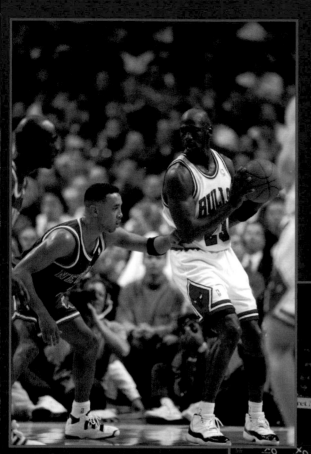

Michael always tried to back me down because he had me by four inches and 35 pounds. I tried to push him back. If I let him cross the line, I was at his mercy. Gary Grant looks on.
Jonathan Daniel/NBAE/Getty Images

Michael's knee brace is finally up over his knee. He always wore it down around his calf when he played for the Bulls. We're just two old fogies going at it.
Kent Horner/NBAE/Getty Images

I wanted to play for the Bulls when I first entered the league, but by the time I finally wore a Bulls uniform, the Bulls were a team in disarray. I wasn't too happy during my short stay in Chicago. *AP/WWP*

I'm driving against the Atlanta Hawks' Hanno Mattola. I thought playing with the Jazz was going to give me another chance to play for a championship, but it didn't turn out that way.
Kent Horner/NBAE/Getty Images

You never know where you'll end up in this league. I always associated Isiah with the Detroit Pistons, but now he's a Knick. *Paul Hawthorne/Getty Images*

CHAPTER 12

EARNING RILEY'S TRUST

"I want John Starks in my foxhole."

—Pat Riley

reg Anthony and I had different personalities, but we became very close. We had different backgrounds, but we still had things in common. Greg had even worked at a Safeway in Las Vegas. He worked as a box boy while I was a checker and then a stocker. The Knicks had signed me to a two-year, guaranteed contract worth $1.6 million. It was a lot more money than I'd ever played for. My lifestyle stayed the same, but when you get that guaranteed money, it takes a lot off your back. Jackie and I didn't have to worry about bills and buying food on sale anymore.

Greg respected where I came from and how I had to fight to make it into the league. Greg had won a national championship playing at the University of Nevada-Las Vegas in 1990. A teammate of his on that UNLV team, Jarvis Basnight, had gone undrafted like me, and he tried out for the Knicks a couple of years later. He was the best player in the preseason camp, but he didn't make the team because all the guys ahead of him had guaranteed contracts. Greg would say, "It's a Catch-22, no matter how well an unsigned player plays, nine times out of ten he doesn't get the opportunity to make a team. John, you beat those odds."

There's a lot of jealousy in the NBA over who's making how much money. Some guys who are making less money than other guys feel that those guys don't deserve to get paid more because their role on the team isn't any bigger. I was never into that. I felt like we were all making a lot more money than most people who work 9 to 5, anyway. We were all making great money, so there should be no jealousy.

When I first started making money in the pros I wasn't making nearly enough to buy my mother a home, but I sent her money and eventually, when I signed my first big contract with the Knicks for $6 million, I added on some rooms to my grandmother's home on Elwood Street and bought my mother a home. It was up in Gilcrease Hills where black folks were trying to move to when I was a kid. It had four bedrooms and my mother and my two sisters moved in. But my mother ended up moving out of it pretty soon after I bought it for her.

My mother didn't like flying, and she wouldn't drive on the highway. When she came out to the home I bought just south of Tulsa, she'd only take side streets and it'd take her 30-35 minutes to get there from North Tulsa when it should've taken her 20 minutes. She didn't like to come to New York because everything was too fast for her. So when my mother got bored, she moved from one house to another. I bought her three different houses and that was her way of dealing with the boredom. She enjoyed decorating, and that kept her busy for a while.

At the start of the 1992-93 season, I became a starter. The Knicks had released Gerald Wilkins, Kiki Vandeweghe and

Xavier McDaniel and traded Mark Jackson to the Los Angeles Clippers for Charles Smith, "Doc" Rivers and Bo Kimble. In addition, Tony Campbell, Rolando Blackman and the rookie, Hubert Davis, joined the team, as did Herb Williams, who became, along with Greg and Patrick and Mase, my closest friends on the team. The thinking was that we needed to get bigger and quicker to beat the Bulls. But we had seven new players and had to find our chemistry.

Even though I was starting, I still didn't know fully what my role on the team was. I knew that by bringing in two guys like Rolando Blackman and Tony Campbell, who had a combined NBA experience of 19 years and had both been 20-point per-game scorers in the league, I was being tested. We had great depth. Riles told me that he liked the way I took the ball to the rim and could also shoot it from deep, but he wanted me to create a move like Ro's and Tony's where I could shoot a nice mid-range, rhythm jumper off the dribble.

So I worked on that move and just did what I always did, ran and lifted and played in the parks. I came into the season ready to play basketball and to compete for a job. If you don't want the competition, you don't need to be in this league. I had to face competition in order to get in the league and I liked the type of situation we had where I had to come into training camp ready to practice and play hard every day. I always thought practice was a lot of fun, because I got to work on my game and square off against my teammates.

As a guard, you have to adjust to your teammates, but it was hard with all those new players. I knew what Patrick liked to do, and he and I started developing more of a two-man game with one another. Coach Riley called most of the plays on offense for us. Patrick loved being on the left block where he could turn to the middle. When he stepped out of the post, I ran the pick-and-roll with him.

When Mase got the ball, I just got out and filled the lane, because Mase could run the break. Mase would find you out there in the open court. He asked me one time, "What do I need to do to get the ball more and bring it up? Send you a Christmas card?" Mase was funny like that. And he could really handle the ball. He was a point guard trapped in a power forward's body.

Oak also wanted the ball, not to bring it up or dribble much, but to shoot his jumpers. Sometimes the Garden fans groaned when he shot too often or from too far out, but Oak's game was the 15-20 foot jumper. He wasn't a post player. He liked to start out high and pass—because he was an excellent passer, too—or shoot or charge in for the offensive rebound. It was Riley's job to make sure everyone got their share of touches. Coach Riley commanded more respect than any coach I ever played for.

We won our first three games of the season, but then we lost four of five and three games straight on a West Coast swing. In the last game of the trip, I got into a trash-talking bout with Mark Jackson out on the court and Riley pulled me and started Blackman in the second half. In the fourth quarter, as I was sitting on the bench, Mark ran by and started talking more noise so I threw a cup of water on him to cool him off. That did not sit well with Coach Riley. He benched me for the next two games.

Mark knew it was all in fun. I didn't have anything against him. When asked to explain why he was benching me—and Greg, too, who had also gotten into the trash-talking with Mark—Riley told reporters, "You can read into that any way you want, but we have to focus and concentrate on playing basketball. You can't let yourself get sidetracked by anything. Starks spent 2 1/2 minutes not playing basketball. That's not what I put him in the game for."

Sitting me down was critical; it helped calm me down. I was having trouble with my perimeter shooting, hitting on only 39 percent of my field goal attempts. I didn't like being benched. I'd played in 130 straight games since the last time a coach's decision had kept me on the bench, and I wanted to keep that streak alive. But I had to realize that my negative emotions were still an obstacle that I had to overcome if I wanted to be a great player.

Doc Rivers told me, "I wouldn't worry about it. I'd hate to be the other team when you get back on the court. The guy you guard is going to catch hell."

Riley didn't start me in the next game, but I came off the bench to hit on nine-for-14 shots and score 20 points in a road win against Minnesota. Then we beat Chicago at home, but we still couldn't get on a roll. We were trading losses with wins. In a home game against Seattle I came off the bench to lead an 18-4 run, and I played my most minutes ever in a game, 37, and scored 18 points.

After the game, Coach Riley said, "John is a guy who comes in off the bench and is going to make something happen. Good or bad, he's going to make something happen. I say that in a very positive sense, because he brings a lot of energy. I don't have a problem with a guy that plays so hard that might play too hard. If he makes a few mistakes because of his effort, we'll applaud that."

I would've rather been starting because it was hard coming off the bench. Just sitting there, you're not warmed up. When I got out on the court, I had to force myself to move and get bumped and just be aggressive in order to get in the flow and get a good sweat going. Basketball is all about rhythm, and I had to shoot the ball a few times and dribble a few times before I felt my rhythm kick in.

When our next West Coast road trip came around, our record was 19-12 and I was still in the shooting doldrums at only 39 percent. I started breaking out of my funk in a home loss to Boston before the road trip. I scored a season-high 28 points on 10-for-20 shooting. We were down 76-53 to the Celtics with 3:58 to go in the third quarter when Coach Riley told us to press full-court and he put me, Mase, Charles Smith, Doc and Ro in the game. We came all the way back, but lost 100-97 when I missed a 25-foot three-pointer with two seconds left that would've tied the score at 100.

Two nights later we played in Sacramento. The Kings had won eight of nine games, but we beat them on their home court. In 28 minutes, I scored a then career-high 33 points on 12-for-16 shooting and had six assists. The basket looked as big as the bicycle tire I used to shoot into as a kid in my neighbor's back-yard on Virgin Street. I always liked playing against Mitch Richmond, because he was an old Big-12 rival from Kansas State, and we had both played on the Warriors together.

After the game, Riles said about Richmond and me, "Those guys are a couple of bulls. I knew John was ready because he went through his pregame ritual where he washes his hands 18 times and just keeps saying, 'We're going to war.'"

The next night in Denver I scored 27 points but we lost. Two nights later in Dallas, we took our second game of the four-game trip, and I poured in 18 points. Three nights later, back in the Garden against the Phoenix Suns, we started a three-month, 39-8 streak to close the season. I hit on three of four three-point shots in the Phoenix game and scored 21 points. Three nights later in Philadelphia, I scored 32 points in 29 minutes. I was on a roll.

Over the next six games, I scored at least 24 points in every game except one and regained my starting shooting guard posi-tion for the rest of the season. Coach Riley started to show a lot more confidence in me. He started me once again in a game against the Hawks at home, and for the first time in my pro career, I played more than 40 minutes (42) in a game, scoring 24 points with eight assists and five rebounds. Over the rest of the season, I played more than 40 minutes in a game 12 times, including 56 minutes in a road loss to the Orlando Magic where I scored 26 points, had eight assists and four rebounds.

On February 4, in a 30-point blowout win against the Warriors, I scored 30 points, and a sell-out crowd at the Garden started a streak of 433 consecutive home sellouts that lasted until January 4, 2002. In a late February game against the Nets at the Meadowlands, Kenny Anderson, the Nets' talented young guard came down on a two-on-one break against me and I put my hands up to try to stop his drive to the basket. Kenny and I collided, and Kenny went sprawling to the floor, but not before he released a shot that went in off the backboard.

The referee called me for a flagrant foul, but I wasn't trying to hurt Kenny, I had great respect for him. And I wasn't trying to send him a message. I was trying to prevent him from getting to the basket. I didn't try to take him out of the air. I was making a play on the ball with my hands in the air. He just hit me with his body and came down wrong. He broke his left wrist when he tried to support himself as he fell.

Rod Thorn, the head of NBA Basketball Operations at the time fined me $5,000 and that surprised me. I thought it was unfair. The only reason I got fined was because Kenny got hurt, which was unfortunate, because the Nets were on their way to a good season and Kenny was having a good season in only his second year in the league. But if he didn't get hurt, there wouldn't have been a fine. Coach Riley called it the most unflagrant fragrant foul he had ever seen.

It was the 11th flagrant foul called against a Knick that season, and the third time the league had fined us. Oak was hit with the other two, totaling $13,500. On one play, Oak blocked Reggie Miller in a play where no foul was even called, but Oak was fined $10,000. If I were trying to flagrantly foul Kenny, his shot wouldn't have gone in the basket. But the flagrant fouls and the fines were something we had to deal with. The league was singling us out.

Almost one month after the Nets game, we played the Suns in Phoenix, and we got into a big brawl. Kevin Johnson spurred it on by hitting Doc with an elbow. I was guarding Kevin at the time and he set a pick on Doc, who was guarding Danny Ainge. Kevin laid one on Doc, knocking him down. Kevin had done it on purpose, so he started running toward the Phoenix bench. Doc took off after him and I was trying to catch Doc so he wouldn't get into a fight. As I was running, Ainge jumped on my back, but I slipped out from under him and got around behind him, and I kneed him in his butt.

I guess Danny didn't like that too much. After he retired and was coaching, he came up to me before a game and told me, "You know, John, I never did like you, but I respect you." I didn't say anything, but I thought, "I can't believe you're telling me this." I took it as a compliment.

Teams were starting to complain about our physical, aggressive style of play. Teams were complaining because they feared us the most out of any team in the league, and the refs unfairly scrutinized us. Doc, Mase, Greg, Oak and I all had flagrant fouls called against us. The other teams wanted to try to distract us from playing our game, and for a while it was in the back of my mind, but I just tried to put it all behind me.

My scoring average was 13.1 points per game and my field goal percentage was .319 at the time of the Boston game, but I upped those marks by season's end to 17.5 and .428, respectively. In a *New York Post* story on January 25, 1993, on the players who shot the most attempts per minute of action, I was listed as the No. 3 shooter, behind Michael and Dominique Wilkins. Michael shot the ball once every 1.52 minutes, Dominique once every 1.70 and I shot it once every 1.94 minutes. At that point in the season, I had played 944 minutes and shot the ball 487 times. Patrick was No. 5 on the list, shooting the ball once every two minutes.

People started calling me a streaky shooter and wondering why I could play great in one half of a game and awful in the next. I think the reason why I didn't shoot such a high percentage was that I took a lot of three-point shots, more than most players did. I'm the Knicks' all-time leading three-point shooter with 982 treys in 2,848 attempts. The league percentage for threes was 34 percent, and I was out there jacking them up. But when I played in college, where the three-point arc was closer in and I didn't take nearly as many of them, my field goal percentage was over 50 percent.

I wasn't the go-to guy, either. Patrick was the go-to guy. If I were going good, Coach Riley would call my plays. So I knew if I got off to a good start, I was going to be in for a big game. But if I didn't start out hot, I had to wait until Patrick did his thing, and sometimes I would just fall out of the offense and take bad shots.

But I also played on an emotional edge. Doc Rivers said I played with a fever. It's the way I learned to play when I played pickup games in the schoolyard. But if I let negative thoughts get into my mind, my shooting and my game suffered.

Coach Riley said my game at that time was "controlled, contained and contemptuous. I can see your shots flying," he told me, "but you still have some contempt for shot selection. When they're falling, I say, 'Good.' Ever since the Boston game you've had it going. I don't care if you take shots—as long as they're in rhythm, with your feet under you, if they come from the post-out and you consider the score and the time. I don't mind you taking shots then, because we need your scoring. It's just that if you miss two or three in a row, you should calm down and get a few lay ups."

But once I knocked down one shot, the feeling came back. I could get on a roll pretty quick—just one good shot, one good look could get me going. And Coach knew I could heat up pretty quickly and he didn't hold me back other than to tell me that the wild shots bothered him, not the amount of shots I took.

When the press asked me about my shooting I told them straight, "Gotta keep shooting. Can't have fear about the misses. You got my job, you gotta keep shooting." I even donned a t-shirt that said, "You miss 100 percent of the shots you don't take."

My daughter Chelsea was born in 1992 and we moved out to a bigger house in Stamford, Connecticut. The NBA puts a lot of strain on your family life because we're on the road the majority of the time. It's especially tough when you have kids and you are not able to spend enough time with your wife and children during the season, which is important. A lot of players get divorces, and that's tough because then it affects your children.

We won 60 games for the season; the first time a Knicks team had done so since the first championship Knicks team of 1969-70, who also won 60. For the record, only six Knick teams in 58 seasons have won 55 games or more, and I was on four of those teams in the 1990s. On April 25, we beat the Bulls at the Garden to reach No. 60.

With six minutes to go in the fourth quarter, I took the ball into the lane with Michael draped all over me and he swiped at the ball. He missed hitting it, but he did hit my middle finger. The finger came out of its socket and it was very painful. I immediately ran over to the nearest bench—it happened to be the Bulls bench—and held out my hand and yelled, "Pop it back in. Pop it back."

The guys on the Bulls bench looked at me like I was a Martian, so I ran over to the Knicks bench and Mike Saunders, our trainer, yanked on the finger and set it back into its socket. I went to the free-throw line, whispered to myself what I always did before shooting a free throw—"Go in, go in, go in"—and I made both of them.

At the end of the game, Michael took a shot at the buzzer and I was still right on top of him even though we had a six-point lead. A reporter after the game asked me why I was still guarding Jordan so tightly when the game wasn't even on the line. "It wouldn't have mattered," he said, "unless Jordan could throw up a six-point shot."

"You never know with Michael," I told him. "You've gotta play him to the end."

Then I told the whole pack of reporters the stance I took when guarding Michael or any other player. "You let him back you up, or you stand your ground. There's the point that you let a player get to, a line, you let him get there and you're his. I've been guarding guys bigger than me all year. I can't let them back me up."

In the last three months of the season I averaged 20 points per game. For the season, I played more minutes per game than anyone on the team except Patrick, even though I hadn't played in two games because of Coach's decision to bench me and I didn't start 31 games. I was named to the NBA All-Defensive second team, becoming the first Knick guard since Walt Frazier and Michael Ray Richardson to make an All-Defensive squad.

I was most proud of that distinction. I tell my own players now as a coach in the United States Basketball League (USBL) with the Westchester (New York) Wildfire that the main thing they can do to get looked at by an NBA team is to play strong defense and stop guys. That's more important than scoring 40 points. Everyone always thought of me as a scorer and many fans when they think of me as a defensive player think about the time Michael scored 55 points against me. But I liked playing defense, and I took pride in it.

One of the tricks of the trade I learned as a defensive player was acting. Sometimes you've got to draw attention to a play by falling down even when you're not hit hard. Sometimes, I'd act like I got shot. When I flopped on purpose, I was trying to draw attention to an offensive player's aggressiveness. If I were guarding someone like Reggie Miller—I'd catch a big man like LaSalle Thompson out of the corner of my eye moving up on me to set a pick—and I'd get ready for that acting job. It was easy to dupe

Getting inside of an opponent's head is part of the game. If I needed to intimidate a player, then that's what I had to do. Oak, Mase, Patrick, and I, we intimidated opposing players. If there was any kind of softness in a player, we were going to find it and exploit it. Mase had a t-shirt that read, "Mase In Your Face."

We won the first two games against the Pacers in the Garden. In Game 2, I outplayed Miller, scoring 29 points to his 25, dishing out 11 assists to his four, rebounding four balls to his one, stealing two balls to his none and even blocking a shot. Coach Riley played me at point guard in the fourth quarter, and on one play I beat the Pacers' forward, Detlef Schrempf, to a loose ball, and as I was falling out of bounds, I threw a strike to Oak for a lay up.

The Pacers were the first team I'd played against that had two really good foreign players in Schrempf and their center, seven-foot-four Rik Smits, who they called, "The Dunking Dutchman." Schrempf was from Germany, and both Smits and Schrempf had played for American colleges, unlike most of the foreign players now in the NBA. But still we felt with guys like Smits and Schrempf that we had to go at them because most foreign players weren't tough defenders.

We were 16 points down in the second quarter of Game 2 when we mounted a comeback. Still down one point in the fourth quarter, I dribbled through the defense for two drives to the basket that led to four points and then I hit a couple of three-point shots. We fought back to win, 101-91.

After the game, Coach Riley told the press: "John played— and I hate to say it, well, I don't hate to say it because he deserves it—he played like an All-Pro. When we got down he played his best. And that's when the greatness of John can come out. He was decisive. He was knocking down shots, he was driving the ball to the basket, he handled the point, he played defense; he has that ability. We've seen enough of that to know that when he's on like that, he's virtually unstoppable."

Even Miller was impressed. Reggie loved to talk trash. It was as much a part of his game as his lethal, long-range outside shot. He was known for it around the league, he even admitted to enjoy being the bad guy. Michael wasn't a talker the way Reggie was. With Michael, when he talked, it wasn't a personal thing. He was just trying to psyche himself up, get himself going. He wasn't trying to diss you like Reggie. It's like Reggie couldn't play basketball unless he was talking. Oak always said, "Reggie's going to talk. That's what he does."

After Game 2, Reggie said, "Starks likes to talk. See, I don't know if he's at that point where he can talk without being distracted. But he's getting there."

When we played the Pacers, nobody else mattered on that team for me except Reggie. I had to concern myself totally with Reggie. He moved without the ball all the time, and their big men: Smits, Dale and Antonio Davis, Schrempf and LaSalle Thompson, all did a good job of setting picks for him. I had to trail him constantly, because I couldn't let him have a smidgen of an opening.

My goal was to always stay close to him so I focused right in on his belly and kept him in front of me. Reggie worked hard on defense, but he wasn't that tough to score on. I agitated Reggie and he agitated me. We were similar players, fierce and aggressive. We both played hard and with a lot of heart.

In Game 3 in Indiana, I hit a jumper to put us up 59-57 in the third quarter when the incident occurred. Reggie came down and hit a jumper with me all over him and he told me all about it as we ran back down court.

"You can't guard me," he said. "Why are you even trying?"

But Reggie's noise didn't get to me. He had been talking to me in Game 2. Reggie had been talking to me from the start of the series. I knew from playing against him over the past few years not to let that get to me. I was ignoring it.

I missed a long jump shot and tried to get the rebound by going through Reggie's legs for the loose ball on the floor and he elbowed me. The next time on offense I got the ball and drove past him and hit a little floater in the lane and Reggie popped me again with his elbow. It was a cheap shot and I could only take so much.

I couldn't let a player disrespect me like that, so I gave Reggie a love tap with my forehead to his forehead just to let him know he had to stop throwing elbows and cheap-shotting me. Unfortunately, Reggie's elbows went unnoticed and I got called for a flagrant foul. Reggie made the play look worse than it really was by falling back dramatically like I hit him with a tire iron instead of my forehead.

The referee called a flagrant foul, level 2, and I got ejected from the game, and the Pacers ended up going on a 30-11 streak with Reggie scoring 36 points for the game. After the head butt, Patrick was hot and he came over and hit me hard in the chest and both he and Oak stood over me and yelled some. My mother called me after the game and told me that she was going to hurt Patrick and Oak for chastising me.

But I knew I'd messed up. I knew how important that game was for our team and they were just being teammates. I blamed myself. I had to take what they doled out. I was a key player and I had to be on the court at times like that to help the team win. I couldn't do that sitting in the locker room.

Pat Riley wasn't happy either. After the game he told the press, "I don't condone that in the least. That's a play that simply shouldn't have been made. John is a front-line player for us. John has to continue to take the responsibility of being a front-line player. You have to have the ability to respond to any tactic by the opposition. If it's physical you have to deal with it. If it's verbal you have to deal with it. You have to stay on the floor and play. We've talked about this all year with our players. The fact that I have to sit here and discuss this, at this time of year after a play-off game, is ridiculous."

Patrick said, "If John doesn't learn how to control his temper, it'll destroy him."

I knew my emotions could get me in trouble. If I was going to be a great player, I couldn't let that physical play get to me. I had to find more self-discipline. But my game relied so much on emotion, my going all out to win, win. You go nowhere in life, you're stepped on if you don't go all out. And I preferred to do the stepping.

The league fined both the Knicks and me $5,000 apiece, but Coach let it go, sort of. A day later he told the media, "You want us to hang him by his thumbs, maybe."

I never felt that I'd gone over the line with Reggie. When it got to the point where his taunting became physical instead of verbal, I had to respond. Verbal is part of the game, and when a player is taunting you and trying to take you out of your game, I could deal with it. But when it became physical, that's something else.

Up until that point in the game, I'd been coping with what Reggie did to me all those years, the little things to piss me off, like being verbally outrageous. I was controlling myself. And so when Reggie saw it wasn't working, he resorted to getting physical with me, elbowing me in the neck, and that was it.

I have no regrets with what I did. And, you know, it served its purpose. Reggie was more careful with me after that game. He knew then that if he got physical with me that I might do something to him. He was right.

Reggie didn't really know who I was at the beginning. And he's the kind of player who unless you gain respect from him, he's going talk to you and intimidate you with his game, but after the head butt, he knew I wasn't going to go for that. Reggie is very competitive, and I respect him for that. But in the NBA, if you let a player disrespect you, then you should take yourself out of the game.

We beat Indiana two days later in Indianapolis, 109-100, to close out the series. I played 43 minutes, compared to the 22 I played in Game 3, and scored 15 points and handed out five assists. I thought the Reggie Miller incident would go away, but I didn't know that in the following two years, the Knicks and the Pacers would face off against each other in two playoff series, each going seven games with Reggie and I right in the thick of both of them.

Then Reggie's book came out in 1994 entitled *Being the Enemy*, in which he said, "I'll tell you right now, I hate the Knicks. Absolutely hate those kids, dirtiest team in the NBA. John Starks made a complete ass of himself in the 1993 playoffs, which is not unusual."

I have to admit during those years I hated Reggie Miller. I hated his talking, his flopping, the way he kicked his leg out on jump shots so that it looked like the defender had run into him and fouled him. But now I look at him out there still playing at 38 years old and still giving it his all and changing his game for the good of his team, and I have great respect for him.

As a coach now of the Westchester Wildfire, I want guys on my team who are winners, who are going to dive on the floor and defend and do the little things to help us win. The guys who are constantly improving are the guys I want on my team, and no one in the NBA wants to win and keeps working on his game as much as Reggie.

The Charlotte Hornets, a strong, young team with Larry Johnson, Alonzo Mourning and Tyrone "Muggsy" Bogues, were next, but we were on a roll and we beat them in five games. The only game we lost, again a Game 3, I played 50 minutes, the last time a Knick has played that many minutes in a playoff game, and scored 19 points, but Muggsy stripped me of the ball at the end as I drove into the lane to try to win the game. In Game 5, the clincher, I scored 20 points and handed out nine assists and we won a tough game at the Garden, 105-101.

The Bulls were next. They were the two-time defending champions and came into the Eastern Conference Finals without having lost a game in the playoffs with sweeps of both the Atlanta Hawks and Cleveland Cavaliers. In the series clincher against Cleveland, Jordan hit a jumper from the right of the key at the buzzer to win the game. Gerald Wilkins, my old tag-team partner against Michael, was guarding him and Dougie was right on the ball, but Jordan's body appeared to float backwards in flight as he shot the ball. Michael had averaged 32.6 points per game in the regular season and had a season-high 64 points in one game.

After the last game of the season when we beat the Bulls and I outscored Michael, Jordan paid me the ultimate compliment when he said about me, "Every time he plays me he seems to be getting better," he said. "He's become a threat."

A reporter asked me before the Bulls series began if I had heard what Michael had said and I hadn't. When he told me, I said with a smile, "Well, that feels good to hear him say that." Then I thought about it for a second and added, "But you also know that's going to make him come even harder."

In Game 2 of the playoffs the previous year, Michael tried to take the game over, and in a span of four minutes he scored 15 points. In the middle of this stretch, he started talking to me and I started talking back, telling him, "No problem, keep shooting, that's what we want you to do." I started telling that to my teammates, too. "You know, I'll stand here and take it because it takes the ball out of the other guys' on his team's hands and then they're not into it during crunch time."

Reporters asked me before the series, "Can you stop Michael?" I told them, "No. All you can do is try to contain him and make him work hard." The thing is, he was the greatest player to ever play the game, and he had me by four inches and about

15 pounds, all I could do was to try to get as much respect from him as I could.

But we were feeling confident with having only two games in the playoffs, and having beaten the Bulls three out of four games in the regular season, including once in Chicago and the last day of the season. Phil Jackson made the comment that our style of play was "basketbrawling" and Michael said, "If Patrick Ewing and Starks are contained, the Knicks certainly are vulnerable. They've had such a tough time scoring."

Coach Riley said, "That's not exactly a news flash," and Oak said, "The Bulls have been saying they want us. But we can't let talk get to us. It's mind games, they're trying to send signals, but they're false signals. We can't listen to them. We've been fired up since we knew we were going to play the Bulls. We're not worried about what people say about us. People want to put us down, but we know we have heart."

I liked the pressure being on me. I've always said you can dream, and I always dreamed about situations like this when I was shooting alone in Cheyenne Park as a kid. I wasn't surprised to find myself on the Knicks getting ready to face off against the Bulls in the Eastern Conference Finals, although I knew a lot of people were. It surprised even some of my own teammates like Doc Rivers, who said, "I thought he was just this wild, crazy guy, but I've never seen a player with the emotional level he has. Some games it hurts him. But not this year."

Two days before the first game on Sunday, Coach Riley said about me, "He's not just a shooter. He's shown us he can be a 12- or 13-assist guy. He's shown us he can get big rebounds. He's shown us he can make four straight free throws, with nothing but net, to win a game. He's shown us he can take it on the drive against three or four guys with tremendous courage. He's shown us he can handle the ball under pressure.

"Much is expected of those who have the talent. John has the talent. Now he has to learn his trade better. It's like a mother eagle nurturing her eaglets. She nurtures, nurtures, and then one day it's time for them to fly on their own."

At the beginning of the fourth quarter in Game 1, we held a five-point lead, 74-69, in a close defensive struggle. I opened up the quarter with three straight threes and we made an 11-4 run. When the Bulls countered with six straight points of their own, I hit a fourth three to give us an 88-79 lead and we won Game 1.

Charles Smith said, "After he hit his first one, I said, 'OK, John is starting to find his rhythm.' After he hit his second, I said, 'OK, John is going to start jacking it.' Then when he hit his third, I said, 'He's unconscious.'"

Michael shot 10 for 27, Mase was all over the court double-teaming and leading the break, and we out-rebounded the Bulls 48-28, pulling down 15 offensive rebounds. Still, after the game the press wanted to know how I did it so I told them.

"There's a determination in me that I can play at this level, and that I can produce. I don't worry about what the public thinks. I just worry about how I can help this team."

Between games 1 and 2, Michael spent all of Monday night and well into Tuesday morning, in an Atlantic City casino. By game time Tuesday night, it had become a big story, but Michael wasn't talking to the media. I didn't think anything about it. I knew Michael would be ready to play.

I thought it was wrong for the press to put him through the wringer like that. That was his free time and what a player does with his free time shouldn't be the public's concern. That's what he did to relax, and people relax in different ways. Some like partying, some like golfing and some like going to the casinos.

Game 2 was even a closer game than Game 1. With one minute left we held a three-point lead, but the Bulls were closing. Patrick and I had been playing together for almost three years by the time I received the ball on the right baseline. I knew what he liked to do to get off his shot and he knew what I liked to do to get mine off. When Patrick set that pick inside of B.J. Armstrong instead of up top, I just followed his lead and took off. I saw the opening and there was nobody in the lane to meet me when I turned the corner.

It was a major play. Some people said it is the single most famous and exciting play in Knicks history and definitely the greatest dunk. The energy that was going through me at the time propelled me into that dunk. It was a great feeling, mostly because it came with only 47 seconds left in the game and it put us up by five points. There's no place like being in the Garden when it's rocking. The fans took me to another level.

When the game ended and we were up two games to none, I felt we were finally on our way to getting over the hump of beating the Bulls and Michael. Even Charles Barkley, who was playing for the Phoenix Suns in the Western Conference Finals against the Seattle Supersonics that year said, "I can't believe he dunked that ball. Shows you the difference between New York and Chicago. I tell you, Michael wouldn't get that play. The Knicks would've knocked him on his butt and not helped him up. I think New York wins the series. I love the Knicks' style because they beat each other up. You got to be a man to play with them boys. Intimidation."

Even some of my own teammates were incredulous. Herb Williams said, "I knew John could go upstairs, but the thing about it is, he brought the ball back to the defense with his left hand. And as high as Michael can jump, you figured he would have gotten it. But he couldn't do nothing with it. John got Michael that day."

A lot of people have talked about that dunk. Pat Riley said it was my unique temperament, an innocence that I had, that enabled me to slam over Michael with the game on the line. Roger Rosenblatt, writing an article on me in *The New York Times Magazine* linked me with players like Dominique Wilkins, Earl

Monroe, George Gervin, Julius Erving and Pete Maravich, saying that I belonged in the "divine" category of the best of players.

"This is the reason for the fans' identification with him," Rosenblatt wrote in 1994. "One minute we are all confined to dismal gravity. The next, there is John Starks in the second game of last year's Eastern finals, suddenly spinning and flying and rising, with four Bulls clinging to him like barnacles, including the greatest great, who had decided to put a stop to the upstart. But the newest of the divines was not to be stopped, because he had not decided anything. He just felt like going to the basket. And he felt like using his left hand, even though he's a righty. And when he posed in the air above the rim, and then pushed the ball through, Oh! how it felt."

And a Knicks fan on his website wrote: "It was the greatest dunk of all time. For that moment, the line separating player from fan was melted as all of New York became a broiling skillet of fanaticism with one single, unified goal, one heart and one soul."

CHAPTER 14

THE COLLAPSE

"Maybe this is the most defining moment of this team's life. We didn't get it done even though we had great opportunities."

—Pat Riley

oach Riley said of the 1993 Knicks-Bulls Eastern Conference Finals series, "John called, and Michael raised." But we still had a very good chance to win the series and beat the Bulls. I ran into trouble in yet another Game 3 of a playoff series, getting ejected just like in the Indiana series. The Bulls were beating us badly in Chicago Stadium when, with 9:09 left in the fourth quarter, Michael and I got into an altercation. I swiped at the ball and accidentally hit his wrist. Then he put his hand in my face and I slapped it down. I wasn't a kid and I wasn't going to take that.

There wasn't any intention on my part to slap him on the wrist. He had injured his wrist earlier in the series and it was still sore. And then I slapped his hand away because he put it in my face. It was a situation where Michael threw an elbow. I said something and he put his hand in my face. I slapped it away and got a tech. I was going to let it go and then it happened a second time, and I slapped his hand down again and I got a second tech.

I knew Michael had the wrist injury and he felt that I tried to intentionally hit the wrist, which I didn't. He had the ball and I just slapped down on the ball, and I accidentally hit his wrist. I think he was frustrated with the whole media situation regarding Atlantic City. When he looked back on it, he probably saw that I was swiping at the ball and not his wrist.

But once again, I was seen as the villain in another Midwest city. I went out to a blues club in Chicago that night with some of my teammates and a lot of people in the club booed when I walked in. I just said to myself, "Someone's got to be the bad guy around here." Coach Riley understood. He wasn't nearly as upset as when the Reggie Miller incident happened because that game was close. This game wasn't.

"He has been rock solid as a player, he has had a great three months for us," Coach told the press. "So we'll put that behind us." But Coach did mention to me that in our nine playoff victories. In 1993, I was averaging 46.8 percent shooting from the field and 18.3 points, 7.8 assists and 1.8 turnovers a game. In our three losses, I'd been ejected twice, shot 35.1 percent and was averaging 10.7 points, 2.3 assists and 4.3 turnovers. He looked me straight in the eyes and said, "John when you're hot, we win. When you're hot-headed, we lose."

In Game 4, even my big effort, 24 points and seven assists, didn't prevent us from going down to Chicago. Michael dropped 54 points on me. We headed home feeling confident, though, because we had knocked off the Bulls twice in the Garden and had a 27-game winning streak there. Patrick played big for us in Game 5, scoring 33 points. We got the ball into his hands at the end of the game down one, 95-94. Everyone in the Garden was on their feet.

Patrick drove to the basket, got tripped and started falling, but as he went down he shoveled a pass to Charles Smith who was standing three feet from the basket. Charles went up and had his shot blocked by Horace Grant, he got the ball back and was stopped by Jordan, he went up again and Pippen blocked his shot, his fourth attempt also got snuffed. The play seemed to take forever. Charles went up and up and up and up.

We were very disappointed to lose that game and our home-court advantage. But we didn't blame Charles. By the time he came to the Knicks, Charles had lost a lot. He had bad knees. They were always sore. The Charles Smith who came into the league probably would've gone up and dunked. He was more of a West Coast player, not a physical, bang-down-low player, and then he lost some of his hop.

I wouldn't say that he was fouled on the play. Even if he was fouled, we were playing Chicago, and Michael and Scottie were doing the defending. The refs were not going to call a foul on those guys on that particular play.

I felt for Charles. I hoped one day he'd have the chance to make up for those plays. We didn't get on him too much for missing those shots because we knew that one day we all might be in the same position. We didn't blame him for the loss. We understood it was a tough situation. That he was playing the fall guy, but the real reason we lost the game was that we didn't shoot our free throws or rebound the ball. I was three for 11 from the field and two of five shooting free throws. Patrick missed six freebies in 14 tries. Oak was two for four from the line and only had four rebounds, and Mase shot one of three from the line.

Back in Chicago, the Bulls finished us off 96-88 and then beat the Phoenix Suns in six games to win their third straight championship. Michael Jordan called it quits and went off to play baseball. I was sad to see him go. I felt that if I could play against Michael Jordan every night, I'd be in heaven.

The fans in New York were upset after that series. I remember there was this one guy who used to wait for us after games down in the parking garage below the Garden, and when I came down to get my car he came up to me. Nowadays, they don't let fans into the parking garage, but back then they did. This guy was a little slow mentally. He said, "John Starks, I love you." I signed an autograph for him and everything, but as I got in my car and started to drive off, he spit onto my windshield. I had to be leery of fans who followed my career so intently that they lived their life through me.

When I would go back to the neighborhoods where I grew up in North Tulsa in the summer, after being in New York all season long, I felt a sense of pride knowing where I came from and what I'd been through. I still belonged to the Greater Union Church that I went to growing up. Over the years it became less a house of prayer and more a house of war. The pastor died and the elders of the church became at odds with one another. Then the youth started to leave and once that happened, the church died. Now they just have a bunch of older people there wondering what happened.

I tried to stick in there as long as I could, but Jackie said, "We've got to go. There's no life here." But that's the church I grew up in. My grandmother used to take us there. You keep your church your home. But the people who were running it couldn't see that by not keeping it up, they were destroying the church. The elders of the church got set in their ways, didn't want to change, and you've got to change with the times, even a church.

I didn't show people up in North Tulsa or treat the people I grew up with any differently than I did before. I was starting to make the money, had nice homes, nice cars, but I treated people the same. I was no different than I was before. If they thought I had changed, it's because they wanted to believe that I had changed. I wanted them to be the same people that they were before when I didn't have anything. But people's attitudes toward you change. They thought that now that I had the money, I must think that I'm something special and that they're nothing. Not everybody thought that way, but certainly some did.

My brothers, particularly Lawrence, would tell me that a lot of people in the old neighborhood weren't happy that I'd become successful. A lot of people resented it because they didn't think that I deserved it. I hadn't been a big star since high school like Wayman Tisdale. Because I was nothing special in high school, people didn't even know my name back then, they wondered why should I succeed and become a professional basketball player?

That's the way it is in the black community. Some people are not going to be happy about your success, but I didn't let it bother me, and I didn't hold it against them. I don't judge them; it's their own issue. It would've been nice if they were happy for me, but I understood that many of them were not feeling too good about their own lives.

I don't get into penny-ante stuff like that. I think it may stem from slavery when some blacks got brought up to the house to work and other blacks had to stay in the barn. That some blacks were getting treated well while others weren't created a divide between black people. It created jealousy and it stayed in the community. As a community, we have to be proud of each other's successes no matter who reaches their goals. But he who finds success also has an obligation to give his time or financial support to programs that help others in the community reach their goals.

The people who knew me and know what kind of person I am knew that I always tried to give back to the community to try to help other people achieve their goals, especially young kids. I think they respected me and they saw that through my endeavors I wasn't only thinking about myself.

I saw myself as just a normal person, and playing ball is what I got paid to do. That's why when I started to get famous, particularly in New York City, at times it bothered me to always be stopped on the streets or in public places. It kind of felt like the movie, *Cape Fear*, with Robert DeNiro, where he's sitting in his car and Nick Nolte comes up to him and tells him to stop bothering his family. Robert DeNiro says, "Man, you're messing with my comings and goings."

I didn't like people messing with my comings and goings either. I like to go in peace and come in peace. Besides, I could do without all the attention. I don't have to have anything like that, but it was nice to be recognized and supported. I always felt supported by the fans when I played in New York, and it certainly has gone a long way now that my playing career is over. But as big as New York is, there seemed no place where I could escape to in the city and its surrounding areas where people didn't know who I was. Everyone is into basketball. Even people you wouldn't think would be into basketball are into basketball in New York.

During my NBA years, Jackie and I went through our ups and downs during those years. We were still young and had only been married for six or seven years. Throw the NBA into the mix, it makes it harder on a marriage. We were in that seven-year itch period and it was itching. One day we had a big argument and the word divorce came up. I had to reach deep down inside myself and think about what getting a divorce would entail. I would've had to leave my wife and my son and daughter. I watched that same thing go on before with my mother and her husbands growing up, and that's another cycle that I had to break. Jackie and I ended up working through our problems.

I got inspiration from reading *Jet Magazine*, especially one article on an older couple that had been married 50 years. I read the story about the older couple's ups and downs and how they got through them, and that helped me. We realized that problems were going to exist, but it's how you deal with them that determines a good or bad marriage. I not only love Jackie, but I am committed to her.

In our profession, the temptation is out there. There are going to be women who want to be with you because of who you are and what you do. I had to understand the consequences, especially for a married man. It's getting worse out there now because of how our big contracts are portrayed in the media. We pick up the paper and read about them and so do the women. We are targets.

The athletes today have it worse than I did, because the money is ten times what it was when I played. They are much more scrutinized; their every move on and off the court is followed. I read in a recent *Sports Illustrated* article that they're talking about players drawing up a contract for a woman to sign before they have sex. It's sad that one day it'll probably come to something like that. It's tough. The temptation out there is very, very real.

The NBA life put a lot of strain on our marriage, but Jackie and I were fortunate to get through the tough times. Jackie is a good woman. She was with me before I made anything, and our strength came from her being with me from the beginning. She struggled along with me when I was cut from Golden State and supported me the whole time. I love her a lot so I just had to fight through it. Temptation is out there. It's definitely out there, and I have been on those long road trips where it hits even harder.

But Jackie was with me through the long haul in our marriage. She knew about my passion for basketball and where it had to take me, and I respect that she was willing to go along with me through thick and thin. She gave up her life to support me, so I want to give as much as I can to her.

Jackie:
My background of coming from a small town helped me in our marriage, because I knew we as a couple would go through a hard time and I just drew back on how I was raised and the moral values I had given. I didn't come from a perfect family, I wasn't perfect, but it was nowhere near the turmoil of John's family. I just had to draw on what was inside of me and say, "You know what, I love him so much, and I'm not going to give up on everything for an unfortunate,

on his part, incident or incidents. I'm not going to give up on what we built all these years, because I know in the natural state, temptation cannot only affect a man, it can affect a woman, as well. I could've said, "That's it. Forget it." But I wasn't going to throw my marriage away for that. Now if it had come to a type of physical abuse, that's a whole different subject.

I was raised in a small-town-girl type of way, and I was always there for John. I didn't go out on the town and stay out late when John was on the road as some of the other players' wives did when their husbands were on the road. I was at home, making sure my kids were taken care of and making sure John had a comfortable place to live when he came back home. I learned this from Chris Riley, Pat's wife, that she made things comfortable for Pat after the game. They're going through a lot, and you've got to be there or there are going to be serious issues down the line.

In eight seasons in New York, I missed onlu four home games. The games I couldn't come to were because a sitter couldn't make it or the weather was so bad I told the sitter to stay home, but I didn't just deliberately not attend a game. When John would lose it on the court, I'd want to crawl under my seat. I'm an expressive person, but I don't necessarily do it before 20,000 people. After the games, I'd stay up late with John and watch the game tape with him, because I knew he'd want to talk about it.

When we moved to New York, I learned a lot about myself. I put up a shield just to guard myself, because I saw so much going on around me I knew that I could get swallowed up by a different value system. I really had to fight that. The temptations were a real struggle. Because we had money, there's the temptation of the flesh; people were drawn to us. Relationships could change at the drop of a hat because there's money and status involved.

After every game in New York, we'd be in our car and fans would chase us down the street for blocks. John would sign autographs for 30 minutes after each game, but then as we attempted to drive off, somebody would say, "There's John Starks," and people would start running after our car. Living in New York was a test, and I *think we did pretty well getting out not divorced and just with our sanity still intact. We came to New York at 24 and 25 years old and we grew up fast.*

I wanted to help Monty, too. I knew he had done so much for me to reach my dreams, but he wasn't around to enjoy my success. I visited Monty in prison as much as I could and gave him money. I would try to drive out to the prison early so that I wouldn't draw attention to myself.

Monty:

I used to talk to John a lot on the telephone. When he first tried out with the Knicks, he'd tell me, "I don't know if I'm going to make it," and I'd tell him, "You just have to play hard." The first time I saw him play on TV, I told everybody, "Damn, that's my little brother," and they all said, "That's B.S., that's not your brother." And I said, "Watch him, he's going to be down here this summer visiting me."

I remember the first time he played against Michael Jordan and I was kind of scared for him, hoping Jordan wouldn't kill him. But John was holding Jordan down. Jordan wasn't going off on him and I said to myself, "Damn, my brother's out there dueling Jordan." I thought, "He's doing a better job than Trent Tucker against Michael. The Knicks need to keep playing John more."

I'd told John that what he ought to do with Reggie Miller is slap the shit out of him one time and let him know you're not messing around with him. Let him know you're for real one time. John knew he couldn't hit him else he'd be suspended for a lot of games and that's probably where the head butt came from.

With Jordan, I told John, if he throws an elbow at you, throw one right back at him. Let him know you're as serious as he is. If he takes your heart from you one or two times, then he thinks that he owns you. Play Jordan just like anybody else. He's no different. Don't shy away from him. Don't let him see any weakness in you. Be a man about it.

I didn't get to see the Knicks-Bulls series of 1993 and John's dunk over Jordan live on TV because McCloud penitentiary, where I was incarcerated at the time, was right in between Oklahoma and Texas and we didn't get NBC. But I saw the highlights of Game 1 and how John was going in and laying the ball up high off the glass and it would hit the rim and bounce off. On one play he had a wide-open lane to the damn basket and he threw the ball up high on the glass. I called him up that night and said, "John, quit doing that damn slimy-assed, soft layup and take your ass in there and dunk."

The guard came in the next night and said, "Boy, your brother went in there and made a spectacular dunk. He went in right over Jordan."

I'm like, "For real?" And he said, "Yeah, man." The next day I saw it on the highlights and I was like, "Damn, this is my little brother! John's all grown up."

A part of me was really happy and another part of me was really mad, because I would've loved to have been sitting in the Garden for that game. When Jordan and the Bulls came back and swept the series, all the guards and a lot of the other prisoners came by and gave me a hard time. I took it pretty hard, but I was still excited about the dunk. It was like John took the lesson I taught him in the playgrounds of Tulsa about going strong to the basket and dunking, and he showed it in Madison Square Garden to Michael Jordan with the world watching.

John used to send me money and I used to have to stretch that money. I still had to take care of my son when I was locked up. John would give me the money so I could take care of my son, Brian. He would tell Brian, "Don't ask me for money, ask your daddy," and John would make sure I had the money, so I could play the father role with my son.

When my son came to visit me I could put money in his pocket so he could buy clothes and tennis shoes. I took care of him. I made sure he had new tennis shoes every month.

CHAPTER 15

STREET FIGHTER TO ALL-STAR

"He was the one person I know, more than anybody I ever played with, that would do whatever it took to win a game."

—Allan Houston, Starks's teammate on the Knicks

In our first two full seasons with the Knicks, Anthony Mason and I only missed three games, not because of injuries, but on Coach's decision to keep us on the bench. Mase was only two years removed from the CBA and I was three years, but in 1992-93, I made the NBA All-Defensive second team and Mase tied for second place for Sixth Man of the Year Award. Entering the 1993-94 season, we vowed in training camp down in Charleston, South Carolina, to keep an eye on each other and make sure that we didn't cost the team in technical fouls, flagrant fouls and ejections.

"It's a big slide back when your game goes up and your attitude doesn't get any better, or if your game's improving and you fly off the handle and do something to hurt the team," said Mase.

"We give the other team, the other players, the edge when we get mad or get techs. That's what they want. If we can play aggressive, play as intense as we usually play, and they say all they want to say and get those cheap bumps and we don't respond, then it bothers them. Then they don't know what to do.

"John and I have worked on improving our games so much, you don't want to be labeled as always jumping in somebody's face or being overly aggressive. After a while, you want to be known as a ballplayer."

I had just turned 28 years old and was a full-fledged starter for the first time on an opening day of the season. Patrick, Oak, Mase, and I, the core of the team, were entering our third season together. Michael, Scottie and Horace Grant were together three full seasons before they won their first championship.

Our practices leading up to the season were fierce. That's always been a hallmark of a Pat Riley team. We all wanted to play a lot of minutes and with guys like Hubert Davis, Greg Anthony, Rolando Blackman, Tony Campbell and Herb Williams on our bench, our practices were probably more competitive than our games. When the regular season began, it was almost a relief. I wanted to win so badly. I could taste the pure thrill of winning. And with Jordan gone, although there was a sense that the league had lost a lot, everyone knew the championship was up for grabs.

Dave Checketts, the Knicks general manager, said, "I think you're going to see the best basketball season ever. Sooner or later, the bloom comes out. There's a cup there to be seized."

We started fast, winning our first seven games, five of which were on the road. Then we lost two in a row. The next game we played Miami in the Garden. I begged Patrick to play that night because he had missed the previous game against Utah with a bad ankle. I had shot four for 21 from the field and was zero for five in three-point attempts against the Jazz, and John Stockton and

Karl Malone gave us our first home loss of the season. But playing with Patrick out on the court was a totally different feeling. The big guy always gave me a feeling of assurance.

Against Miami, I started off cold again. But then suddenly, I got hot. I hit a three from the left corner; another from the right corner; a third from the top of the key; another with someone's hand in my face. I even banked in a 25-footer as the 24-second buzzer sounded. After a breather on the bench to start the second quarter, I hit another three to tie the NBA team record for three-pointers made in a half. With less than a minute to go in the second period, I sunk the three-pointer that broke the team record and tied an individual record of seven in one half shared at the time by John Roche and Michael Adams, both of the Denver Nuggets. I had 31 points in the first half, on seven for eight threes, and we were way ahead.

But with 20 seconds to go in the first half, Brian Shaw stripped me of the ball and I chased him down the court and got ahead of him and tried to draw an offensive foul. He came down on me and his elbow accidentally hit my nose and broke it. I knew it was broken right away because I was in a lot of pain at that particular point. The bone of my nose was actually protruding through my skin.

I went back into the locker room at halftime and got the plastic mask that was made for me the year before when I also broke my nose and came out to play the second half. We won the game, but I wasn't very effective in the second half, scoring only six points and not hitting another three. Brian Shaw's record at the time of eight three's in a game was safe.

I was like a boxer I guess. Doc said after the game, "John played with such effort. The play when he broke his nose, at that point, we were up by 22 points and he still runs down, tries to draw an offensive foul, and breaks his nose. That's John Starks for you."

Coach Riley said, "He's a tough kid. He showed character today. The skin was torn off the nose."

My feeling about playing with injuries was that if the injury just caused pain, I'd play through the pain. But if the injury affected my play, then I'd sit down. I always wanted to compete, but only if I could help the team. I didn't like taking painkillers or medication. I have a high tolerance for pain. If I had dislocated fingers or shoulders, broken noses, sprained ankles, I usually just played. I was never sore after games and I didn't like lying on training tables.

We continued to roll. We won 15 of our first 19 games, and I was averaging more than 19 points a game. I was shooting 42 percent from the field while shooting nearly six three-pointers a game. Coach called most of the plays for Patrick and me. Oak complained sometimes that he never got plays called for him, and the only way he got the ball was by going in and getting it off the glass, but he was like everybody else on the team from Ewing to Mase, Charles Smith, Hubert, Derek Harper, Blackman, Herb and me. We'd all either been big scorers in college or the pros, so we all liked to shoot.

Derek had come over from the Dallas Mavericks in a trade for Tony Campbell when Doc went down with a knee injury. Harp brought a lot of intelligence and experience to our team. He knew how to run an offense, could knock down big shots and on any given night could score 20 points. The only guy who didn't shoot much was AB, Anthony Bonner, and that's probably why during the regular season, he had by far the highest shooting percentage on the team, well over 50 percent.

But Oak was something else. When I shot the ball too much and started missing, Oak had this counter in his head of how many shots I'd taken and he'd tell me, "You're missing too much. I'm not passing you the ball." One time in one of my more erratic games, Oak was passing the ball in from out of bounds under our basket when a fan yelled out, "Don't give it to Starks." Oak said, "I won't." Oak just did his own thing.

You didn't want to get on Oak's bad side. Oak is not the kind of person who just lets things slide. When you cross him, you cross him forever. He has the memory of an elephant and it doesn't matter if you forget about a fight, he doesn't, and he's going to get you back. Once you cross him, you cross him. Oak and Charles Barkley had some run-ins early on in their careers and neither one liked each other. It was part personal and part competitive, but it got worse when Oak came over to the Knicks from the Bulls and Barkley was starring for the Philadelphia 76ers. Oak would never let it go. To this day he doesn't like Barkley and won't talk to him even if he sees him in public.

Getting open looks for shots became harder for me as teams tried everything to take me out of my game. Coach Riley said to me, "They trap you on pick and rolls. They stunt three guys out on you on catch-and-shoot plays. They never leave you alone anymore on double teams. You're drawing a lot more attention, so you've got to learn to make more plays for other people."

I went through a really bad stretch in December where over eight games I shot 41 for 125 (.328) from the field, including six for 40 (.150) on three-pointers. It was probably the toughest stretch I'd endured since I'd been with the Knicks. I was thinking too much. As a shooter, you have to understand yourself. I just had to play and not think about shooting when a shot presented itself. Coach Riley pointed out that I wasn't squaring up and getting balanced on my shots, that I was drifting on my shot. That was the biggest reason why I would miss, or because my shooting wrist would fall off to the side on my release.

Coach got upset with me after a loss to the Nets when I shot two quick three-pointers in the last 1:13 seconds and missed both. He told me, "Those shots were so bad, John, they actually could be classified as turnovers. You have to think about time, score and shot clock before you shoot." He was also angry with Patrick for trying to shoot a long turnaround-jumper over Derrick Coleman at the end of the game instead of kicking the ball out. In practice the next day, he lectured the entire team.

"It all comes down to trusting one another at the end of the game. Can I trust you as a team in critical situations to do what we drill every day? Will you trust one another that you will make the right play and leave the team with the best shot available?

"That's what poise is about: trusting your teammates and trusting the situation because you've been in it before. We always have had a tendency on this team not to trust one another."

Coach was right. We probably didn't trust each other in certain instances. We all knew our flaws as a team. We weren't a good transition team and that put a lot of pressure on our half-court offense.

I was also doubling as the backup point guard, and my shooting problems began to affect the rest of my game. I had eight turnovers in two games and my teammates started calling me "Apple Turnover." The whole team was playing loose with the ball, and Coach made us practice passing and catching with two hands and then he lectured us about that. Whether it was a post-practice or pregame talk, Coach always seemed to have a scripted speech ready.

"One of the most difficult things for you to do," he told the whole team, "is pass the ball with two hands and catch the ball with two hands. It's very basic, rudimentary basketball. We've got two hands and we never try to use them. We try to catch it with one hand and try to throw it with one hand. I think if we just try to catch and throw passes with two hands, we'll cut out six turnovers a game.

"To become a better team we're going to have to become more fundamental. And it's not uncool to throw two-handed passes. It's not uncool to catch with two hands. If you take it for granted as a pro—everyone's catching it with one hand and palm-ing it out here—sometimes you get carried away with that and you don't make the play that's there to be made. You work too hard defensively to get a three-on-one break to not complete it with a layup or two free throws."

I was shooting a lot more than I ever had. In the first 38 games of the season I shot more than 20 shots in a game 17 times. In a home win against Orlando in January, I matched my career-high 39 points on 13-of-29 shooting from the field. I guess I liked shooting a lot of shots against the Magic, because I shot the ball 36 times against them in a game the previous year, one of only two times I ever shot more than 30 shots from the field in a game.

One month later, playing Orlando again at the Garden, I entered the game in the fourth quarter with the Knicks holding a shaky 75-70 lead. Up till then, I had missed 10 of 14 shots. But when I came off the bench, I knew it was time for me to take over the game. I hit a three-pointer from the left side to put us up 82-73 and then moments later, I made sure my sneakers were set inches behind the three-point arc, and I hit another three and we went on to win, 95-77. It's like Larry Bird said, the three-point shot could stop momentum. It seems to play mind games with the other team.

Along with Patrick and Oak, the coaches voted me onto the 1994 Eastern Conference All-Star team. The game was played in Minnesota in February and it was Patrick's eighth appearance in an All-Star game, but the first for both Oak and me. I became the first NBA All-Star ever to have come into the league as an undrafted player and the first ever to have also played in a CBA All-Star game.

I played 20 minutes in the All-Star game and scored nine points. In our second game after the All-Star break, I scored 32 points and dished out seven assists against Cleveland in a road win, hitting on 13 of 15 of my shots and all three of my shots behind the three-point arc. The next game we beat the Bulls at home, and then two days later we beat Seattle with Gary Payton and Shawn Kemp, and I scored 30 points. The ball was in my hands a lot, and that's the way I liked it. I was averaging 19.4 points per game and leading the team in assists and three-point shots. I was playing the best basketball of my life.

Coach Riley told the press, "Teams are playing John like Michael Jordan, and that's the truth. They get in his face. They deny him. They switch out on him. They don't let him catch and shoot the ball. On pick-and-roll plays, he's developing great sense. He's leading the team in assists the last nine or 10 games with seven, eight, nine assists a game. He's making plays for people. Somewhere along the way, if he keeps playing the game and lets the offense come to him, he'll get open for some threes."

Sixteen days after the Seattle game, in a road game in Atlanta on March 14, 1994, I was running back on defense to try to stop a fast break when I turned quickly and my left foot slipped from underneath me and I twisted my knee. I came out of the game, but I didn't think I'd hurt my knee seriously. I thought I'd just tweaked it.

It was sore that night so I kept icing it. We took a flight to Boston that night for a game the next day and when I got to the hotel and took off my pants, my knee had blown up like a grapefruit. I flew back to New York alone to see the Knicks team doctor, Norman Scott, to find out the extent of my injury. Except for the time I had sprained my left knee in the collision with Patrick, I had never experienced a serious injury before.

Dr. Scott told me that I had torn cartilage in my knee and that I needed surgery. Days before my surgery I was outside for four hours with a sledgehammer ounding on this big mound of ice that formed in my driveway, pondering if I would make it back for hte playoffs that year. Four days after the diagnosis, the surgery was performed at Beth Israel Hospital in Manhattan. Dr. Scott did not have to remove the cartilage; he found that he could repair it, which was a major blessing, because I would still have the natural cushioning of the cartilage in the knee to prevent further injury. I left the hospital on crutches the next day after eating a hamburger and a milkshake. Dr. Scott told me the injury would require at least six to eight weeks of healing. That was a problem because the playoffs started in exactly five weeks and six days from the date I had my surgery.

We had a four-game winning streak when I went down with the knee injury and the team proceeded to win 11 more straight games. I worked real hard on my rehab to strengthen the knee, one exercise I did again and again was to have a heavy sled tied around my waist and then walk up and down the hospital hallway dragging it. During games, I sat on the bench and cheered on my teammates. Derek Harper and Hubert Davis were playing particularly well, but my teammates all urged me to get ready for the playoffs.

Hubert told the press, "We can't win a championship without John," and Anthony Bonner said, "John is our emotional leader."

The playoffs are their own little season. The competition is so much more intense than the regular season. The game slows down, and defense is everything. Players who can have big scoring nights and who can create their own shot or create a good shot for a teammate are that much more valuable in the playoffs because there are no easy buckets.

I thought I was physically ready when the playoffs came around, but I had no lift. I'd lost a lot of my explosiveness and I couldn't go up and dunk over big men. I used to be able to take off from behind the dotted line in the lane and dunk, but coming back from the injury I was barely able to dunk at all. I couldn't go around defenders and get to the basket the way I was accustomed to and had taken for granted before the injury.

But playing with injuries, fighting through injuries, was the only way I knew how to play the game. Growing up, when I watched pro basketball, it seemed to me that all the good players played with injuries. I always thought one of the qualities that separated a great player from just a good player was to play hurt.

CHAPTER 16

LIVING FOR THE PLAYOFFS

"John wasn't blessed with any one great skill, but he had such unusual hustle and heart. People who say his career was about two for 18 should be ashamed. What they forget is, with four weeks to go in the regular season, John had knee surgery that year. He was back in time for the first playoff game. Think about that. His pain threshold and his desire were so high."

—Jeff Van Gundy, Starks's last coach with
the New York Knicks

The first playoff series was against the Nets and in the first two games in the Garden, I barely got off the bench, playing nine minutes in the first game and 21 minutes in the second. I scored a total of nine points in the two games. Riles said he felt it was a risk to work me back into the lineup during the playoffs when I'd missed the last six weeks and 23 games of the season, but to tell you the truth, I was mad that I wasn't starting. I remember thinking to myself, "Why isn't Coach starting me?"

The Indiana Pacers and Reggie Miller awaited us in the Eastern Conference Finals. Indiana had lost only two games in the first two rounds of the playoffs against the Magic and the Hawks, but we beat them handily in the first two games of the series at the Garden. Larry Brown had replaced Bob Hill as the Pacers coach and the Pacers were a very balanced team with six players averaging in double figures during the regular season, led by Reggie's 19.9 points per game.

It never bothered me who an opposing team's coach was. Phil Jackson, Larry Brown, Pat Riley or Don Nelson, it didn't matter. I never felt a coach made much of a difference in a game. A coach's most important job is putting a team together and that happens before a season starts. If you look at the Lakers five years ago when Del Harris was coaching the team, they couldn't get it done even with Kobe and Shaq. Phil Jackson, with all his championship rings and his knowledge of the game, brought in a level of respect and he changed that team. The coach's job is to orchestrate, but it's still the players' game once the referee tosses the ball up for the opening tap.

The Pacers beat us in Games 3 and 4 in Indiana and then back at the Garden in Game 5, when Reggie went off in the fourth quarter scoring 25 points, 37 for the game, the Pacers won again, 93-86. We headed back to Indiana for Game 6 where the Pacers had been 29-12 in the regular season and hadn't lost a game in the playoffs. Our backs were up against the wall.

We couldn't let our championship hopes die in Market Square Arena. This was it for us. It wasn't about Reggie and me. It was about two teams, and one of us was going to the Finals. The night before the game, I called a players-only meeting in Patrick's room because he had the suite. I felt we needed to get everyone on the same page and Monty had called me saying that I should do it. He also told me that I had to tell Oak to switch out on Reggie when one of Indiana's big men cut me off with a pick.

We needed for all of us to get on the same page and watch film. Riles always said, "the film doesn't lie." The meeting helped a great deal because when we got to talking we all mapped out what we were going to do. "Listen Pat, when I throw the ball into you, and they do this, we're going to be over here." That kind of stuff. We all got focused on our jobs.

As soon as we walked out of the tunnel in Market Square Arena and I saw Spike Lee seated at courtside, across from the Indiana bench, I knew we were going to win. In the biggest game of my life up to that point, I scored 26 points on eight-for-11 shooting. I went five for five on my threes and I dished out six assists. We beat the Pacers in their own building, 98-91. I bothered Reggie into shooting eight for 21 from the field. By the end of the game, I knew both Reggie and I were tired. Our defense won the game. I just got down low and fought through all the screens. All of us were more aggressive.

Coach took me out with three seconds left in the game and us holding a six-point lead. As I reached the Knicks bench, I paused and looked up at the screaming Indiana fans. I raised my hands up over my head and waved at them to scream and boo and swear some more. Then I turned my back on them and plopped back into my folding chair. We were going home to the Garden for Game 7 with a chance to play in the NBA Finals.

I don't think I ever saw Riles so pleased. "There was a massive, massive thud the other night with everyone jumping off our bandwagon," he told the press after the game. "We may not be the prettiest team around, and we may not be the most skilled. But I can't understand the questioning of this team's heart. This team is all about heart. That is what has gotten us here."

The victory over Indiana in Game 7 of the Eastern Conference Finals at the Garden was the greatest feeling I ever experienced as a professional basketball player. A Dale Davis dunk put the Pacers ahead 90-89 with about 45 seconds to go.

We called a timeout to set up the pick-and-roll play for Patrick and me. I had the option of either coming off the pick and passing the ball to Patrick or taking the ball to the basket. I saw the opening and drove the ball for a twisting lay up that bounced off the backboard and rolled off the front rim. Patrick swooped in and jammed the ball in with two hands and 26.9 seconds left.

Up 91-90, I was exhausted from having played 81 minutes in two games over three days. Indiana had the ball, trying to go ahead and they were looking to Reggie. Dale Davis came down to the baseline to set a pick, and Reggie ran me into him as he came around the left wing looking for the ball.

We were a defensive team primed on calling out picks and making switches. I called out to Oak, who was guarding Davis, "He's coming your way, Oak. He's coming your way." Oak got out quickly and put a hand in his face, and Reggie shot an air ball.

Before we could even inbound the ball, Reggie knocked me to the floor and Mike Mathis called a flagrant foul with four seconds left. I made three free throws to end the game and we won, 94-90.

The Garden crowd went crazy. I looked over at Coach Brown and he was disappointed. When I looked at the tape that night, I saw that Jeff Van Gundy couldn't even look up when Reggie took that last shot. He was sitting with his hands over his eyes. I felt so good for Patrick because he had a huge game, scoring 24 points with 22 rebounds, seven assists and five blocked shots.

"It was a long time coming," Patrick said after the game. "I wanted the ball in my hands down the stretch. I mean if we lose, I'm the one who gets blamed anyway."

I said, "The big fella wouldn't let us lose tonight. I told Patrick the whole game, 'Keep coming to the basket, baby,' because I knew he would get the rebounds. Actually, I thought I had made the last shot, but then I saw Patrick soar and put it back in."

I scored 17 points and was one of five Knicks who scored in double figures. We out-rebounded the Pacers 59-38. Anthony Mason said after the game, "We like to do it ugly. If we won in four or five games, it wouldn't be the Knicks. We like flirting with danger."

CHAPTER 17

NO FEAR

"Live your life so that whenever you lose, you are ahead."

—Will Rogers

We had two days between the end of the Indiana series and the start of the Finals in Houston. We were all exhausted having played two straight seven-game series. My uncle Frank had died, and I flew back to Tulsa for the funeral, missing the Monday afternoon practice in New York. Uncle Frank was married to my Aunt Ora, my grandmother's sister. We used to live down the street from them on Virgin Street.

The first game in Houston was the 41st day since the start of the playoffs and our 19th game. Counting the regular season, it was our 101st game of the year. We were tired and we had to change gears some, because Houston was an entirely different team than Chicago and Indiana. We felt that we were much more physical than Houston. Seattle was the best team in the West that year, but they had been knocked off in the first round by the

Nuggets. The Nuggets were beaten by the Jazz, who lost in five games to the Rockets in the Western Conference Finals. The Rockets had never won an NBA Finals, in fact Houston was known as "Choke City." The Knicks hadn't won a championship in 21 years, not since Reed, Frazier, DeBusschere, Bradley and Monroe.

I never once talked to any of those guys from that 1973 team about their perspective on winning championships. We were two teams from different eras. They would've loved for us to talk to them about that kind of stuff, but we were young players, and we thought we had all the answers. I think it would've helped to talk with Walt Frazier, Earl Monroe and Reed about what it took to win a championship, but all I ever did was look at the pictures on the Garden walls of their championship seasons.

When I came onto the court in the Summit for the pregame warm ups for Game 1, I thought the game was seriously over. I thought we would definitely win. I felt good. We were the more experienced team. Besides Olajuwon, Otis Thorpe, Vernon Maxwell and Kenny Smith, all the rest of the Rocket players were young and virtually untested in the playoffs. But their young players, Sam Cassell, Robert Horry and Carl Herrera, ended up playing very well.

The media made a big deal about my matchup with Maxwell, calling him "Mad Max" and me, "The Wild Thing." Vernon and I had come up together with the San Antonio Spurs in 1988. I guess they saw a comparison between our emotional style of play, our fire and our long-range shooting. Max had hit 120 threes in the regular season, and I had made 113. But I never focused on personal matchups. Basketball is a team game; you can't compare it to the matchup between pitchers and hitters in baseball.

I played poorly in Game 1, shooting three for 18. But we were still in the game at the end, only down three, 79-76, when I pulled up for a three with Maxwell in my face and shot an air ball. We lost 85-78.

After the game, Riles wasn't happy. "I don't know if John should have pulled up for a three," he said. "He has hit those before for us, but we wanted to drive the ball to the basket."

In Game 2, I rebounded with 19 points and nine assists and we took away the Rockets' home-court advantage with a road win. I rarely played poorly two games in a row. After the first game, I sat in my hotel room and meditated on what I had to do, and then I came to the arena early and took a lot of warm up shots.

Riles said, "The series doesn't get interesting until the home team loses."

As a team, we shot 52 percent and held the Rockets to 83 points. Riles said, "Our defense is only as good as the pressure we put on the ball," and Maxwell definitely felt it, because he said, "This was a hard night of work. They were playing us straight up. I hate that. I wasn't getting the open looks I normally get."

Derek Harper had 18 points and made life miserable for Kenny Smith. Derek said to me, "In the previous series, they faced guys who sagged a lot on defense. I don't think they're used to playing under the kind of pressure that we're capable of putting on people."

Game 3 back at the Garden was the game that broke our backs. Big games like that one are what I lived for. At three o'clock I'd finish dinner and lay out the clothes I'd wear to the Garden and get ready for the drive into Manhattan from Stamford. Jackie knew that I started to change around that time of the day. I'd start getting my energy and competitiveness up. From the moment I got into my car to drive to the Garden, it was like I was a different person.

Driving into the city I'd listen to jazz with no lyrics just to get my mind right. The first turn driving up Seventh Avenue, when you see the sign, "Madison Square Garden," that said it all.

When I got into the building, that's when I began to sweat. That building is out of this world. The fans. Chicago is loud, but not like New York. It's totally different; I just don't know how to describe it. The Garden was a pressure-cooker place to play. Every day you had to go out there and perform. But the playoffs were a different level; the crowd was very electrifying. I never felt a rush walking into any other arena like I did coming into the Garden. The fans got really into the games. No other team's fans matched the Garden's for intensity.

I'd put on my uniform and go out before warm ups and shoot jumpers from the spots on the court I tended to shoot from in the games. Then I used to go into the little trainer's room where we used to get checked for injuries and close the door and turn off all the lights. I'd lie on the trainer's table and it'd be completely dark in there, and I'd get myself focused. I'd think about who I was going to play against, the guy I was going to guard.

The locker room would be filled with people and everything would be going on around me. I would kid with my teammates, the media came in to interview us, players would get taped up for the game by the trainers, but that little trainer's room is where I got some quiet time. For 15 minutes, before it was time to go out on the floor, I'd go in there and block everything out and visualize what I wanted to do out on the court.

It was working to plan in Game 3. I was having another big game and we were up by two in the closing seconds when Sam Cassell scored the last seven points of the game for the Rockets and hit a crucial three that put them up 89-88 with 28 seconds left. On that play, Derek was guarding Cassell, and I was up top with Vernon. Someone passed the ball into Hakeem in the post and he turned into the paint and acted like he was going to shoot. We were all saying, "Stay home, stay home," because we knew that a lot of the time Hakeem kicked the ball out to a shooter. Derek got caught looking and cheating down to the foul line and Cassell walked right into a three-pointer.

We had the ball and a chance to win the game, but Patrick got called for an illegal screen as he tried to free me up to take the last shot. I was hot, having scored 20 points on six-of-11 shooting with nine assists. Patrick was hot after the game, screaming in the locker room, "You can't make a call like that in our building at that point in the game."

Game 4 we won pretty easily, 91-82, the nine-point margin was the biggest of the series. Game 5 was played on June 17, 1994, and that date was historic for more than just our victory over the Rockets that put us one game away from winning a championship. Houston led 79-76 with 4:26 to go in the game, but I hit a three with 2:22 left that put us up 81-80, and we went on a 7-0 run to put the game away.

The Rangers had won the Stanley Cup just three days before, snapping a 54-year championship drought, and had held their ticker-tape parade through Manhattan on June 17. But June 17 is also known nationwide as the afternoon O.J. Simpson led the Los Angeles police on a 50-mile, slow-ride chase down a Southern California highway on his way to visit his mom. Al Cowlings, his old Buffalo Bills teammate, drove the white Bronco while O.J. was in the back holding a gun to his head.

Since we didn't win another Finals game after June 17, people later made jokes that we lost the series because of O.J. But for me, June 17 was just another day. It never mattered to me which celebrities were sitting in the seats at courtside, and in those days there were a lot of them—from Spike to Woody Allan to MC Hammer—or which ones NBC cut away to during our game riding in a white Bronco. When I stepped on the court I didn't notice any of them. But what happened with O.J and more recently, what's happened with Kobe, is sad. Athletes are in the spotlight and we should understand that. The fame and the notoriety come with the territory.

As a professional athlete, you're only as good as your last game. One minute, the fans are cheering for you and the next they're booing you. Image-wise, it only takes a millisecond to mess up your career by decisions that you make off the court.

After the game we couldn't wait to turn on the television set to see what happened with O.J.

Some guys may believe that what they do or did in the athletic arena makes them exempt from whatever trouble they get into in real life, but I never thought that way. Certain guys got in to trouble when they were younger and got away with quite a bit because of their athletic glories, but as you get older that attitude comes back to hurt you, because now you're playing for keeps. When you're younger, it doesn't mean anything. But when you're an adult, you're dealing squarely with the law.

You get to a certain point in your life where you have to grow up and some people unfortunately never do. I reached that point when I got kicked out of junior college and started living with Monty and selling drugs. I started praying to God to help me and I started thinking more seriously about what I was doing and I began to make better decisions. I was going through tough times and I didn't fully understand what was going on around me. It was easy to make mistakes then, especially because I didn't have the right people around me then to guide me. But I learned from the mistakes I saw Monty make and I learned a lesson from Monty about what not to do.

We were one victory away from winning the championship and staging the second parade down Broadway in one week. Patrick wasn't having a big offensive series, because the Rockets were double-teaming him, but he had blocked eight shots in Game 5, tying the NBA record for blocked shots in a playoff game. After the game, he said, "I've won a championship at every level except one. This is the last one I need to get."

The Garden crowd sent us back to Houston with a chant of "Knicks in six." All there is to tell about Game 6 is that it came down to one play. With 7.6 seconds left to play, we were down two, 86-84, and we had the ball on the left sideline out of bounds. Oak inbounded the ball to me and I had three options: drive, pass the ball to Patrick or shoot a jumper. Riles left the decision up to me.

Horry committed a foul, so we inbounded again with 5.5 seconds. Patrick set a pick on Maxwell, and all I thought of was going for the win. I took two dribbles to my left and fired and when the ball left my hand, it was money. I didn't even think of Hakeem getting to it.

In hindsight, I should have told Patrick not to come and set the pick so I could have gone one on one with Maxwell, which would have kept Hakeem away from the play. I was on fire, so if I had gotten the shot up, it was going in. I asked Patrick after the game if he was open when I came off the pick and he said he was.

Derek told me on a last-second shot like that, it would've been better if no pick was set at all. That way I could've broken my man down with the dribble and gotten off a better shot. I heard some TV announcer say after the game that there couldn't be a storybook ending because these were Pat Riley's Knicks, but I saw the opening and I thought I could knock the three-point shot down.

I wanted to win the game. Hakeem simply made a great play. I had a great look at the basket and probably no other center in the game could have made that play. As a player you make a judgment, a decision, and you have to follow it. I have to live with that play and knowing that if I had gotten that shot up, the champagne would've been popping in our locker room and all over New York City.

I scored 16 of the team's 22 points in the fourth quarter, but I couldn't hit the biggest shot of my life, and for the next couple of days, that shot was virtually all I thought about. The Rockets' coach, Rudy Tomjanovich, said, "I just have to give John Starks a lot of credit. This guy, he's amazing. There's a little crack in the defense, and it's only there for a split second, and this guy is getting them off." But I couldn't stop thinking of the last shot that I couldn't get off.

A lot was made out of Mase and me not talking to the press the day before Game 7 and how we were fined $10,000 apiece and the team an extra $20,000. Oak even said about me, "Some guys can't handle this. A couple of years ago, he talked to everybody. Barbara Walters. Doctor Ruth, whoever." What I couldn't stand was repeating the same answers to the same old questions. I had talked to the press after Game 6 and after practice the next day. What else could I have possibly said different the day before the game that I hadn't already said before? They were just going over the same stuff. I'd answered their questions twice, but they kept asking the same questions. Enough is enough.

In hindsight, I probably should've gone in and talked to the press the day before the game because the fine did distract me. I should've handled it like Rasheed Wallace did when after a tough loss, he answered every question asked of him with: "Both teams played hard."

In Game 7 I just let my emotions get the best of me. I was so restless the night before that game. I just couldn't stop thinking about winning a championship. I just wanted it so badly. I thought we were going to win, because all through the series, we'd been swapping losses and wins. I felt it was time for us to win and I was too overconfident. Usually before big games, I had that fear of losing. If you don't have that fear of losing, you don't have that edge. You have to have that fear of losing like we did in Indiana in Game 6. The fear of losing always made me play harder.

A lot of people criticize Coach Riley for sticking with me too long in Game 7 and not replacing me with Hubert or Rolando, but he was staying true to himself as a coach. Riles believed in me, he believed in my ability to hit big shots in big games. I had done it in the 1994 Playoffs in Game 6 against Indiana, Chicago Game 7, and Games 2 through 5 in the Houston series. In Game 6, I shot only two for eight in the first half, and entering the fourth quarter I had scored only 11 points and I still ended up with 27 points. But I found myself pressing in Game 7, trying too hard to make things happen.

A lot of people said that the reason I felt I had to score so much was because Patrick didn't hold his own against Olajuwon.

But we were playing Hakeem straight up with Mase, and a six-foot-eight man can't stop a great seven-foot center like Olajuwon. Patrick got double-teamed that entire series. He didn't have a great series offensively, but I don't think it was because he felt intimidated by Olajuwon, like some people said. There was a history between Patrick and Olajuwon going back to when they played in the 1984 NCAA championship game and Patrick's team, Georgetown, beat Olajuwon's team, The University of Houston.

Patrick made big shots in big games. He made the biggest shot when I missed that lay up in Game 7 against Indiana and he swooped in to dunk the ball. He hit a lot of big shots over the years. A team is asking a lot of a big man when it expects him to hit big shots. Normally, that's the role of the guards. Patrick and I knew each other's game and respected one another immensely. We had lockers right next to each other. I never played with or against a center who played with the ferocity and heart that Patrick did.

Playing the way I did in a key game like Game 7 at Houston I felt was inexcusable. I blamed myself for the loss. I sat in the locker room for a long time afterward thinking. The feelings I had I can't really even explain today. All I kept thinking was, "It's over!" And I couldn't believe it. I thought we were going to win the ball game. I thought we were going to win the series.

People said that it wasn't a very enjoyable Finals to watch, because it was the first time since the shot clock had been put in that neither team reached 100 points in any game of the series. But I thought it was a good Finals. It was a defensive struggle. Whichever team burst out with an offensive spurt won the game. We were the two top defensive teams in the league with two great shot-blockers. Whenever you have a matchup like that, you're not going to see pretty, graceful, athletic games.

Coach Riley had been involved as a player in the great Knicks-Lakers Finals of the 1970s and as a coach in the Lakers-Celtics Finals of the 1980s and he said about the 1994 Finals:

"This is as close a series as I have ever been in. There was not one game that got away from anybody. I can remember getting blown out in Boston and Detroit. Each and every one of these games has been decided in the last three or four minutes."

I think both the Rockets and Knicks of 1994 would've beaten either the San Antonio Spurs or the New Jersey Nets of 2003, the two teams who played in the 2003 NBA Finals. All of their games except the first one were also played in the 80-90 point range. I think in the playoffs when the game slows down to a snail's pace and half-court offense prevails, I think we would've been too tough for either of those teams.

If the 1994 Knicks played the 2004 Detroit Pistons, it would be an outright war. Think of the match-ups. Derek Harper versus Chauncey Billups, me and Richard Hamilton, Oak and Ben Wallace, Patrick and Rasheed Wallace. That would be a hard-played series.

CHAPTER 18

FAMILY TIES

"Tulsa is home. We're a very close-knit family and John has ties to his people back here. All we had growing up was each other and love."

—Lawrence Peoples, "Ju Ju," John's youngest brother

I was very fortunate to play for the Knicks and in the spotlight, especially during those years when Pat Riley was the coach and we played so many games on national television. My brother Tony saw a lot of games at the Garden. My grandmother and mother even made it up to New York on occasion to see me play. Callie West came up for the 1994 playoffs and sat in my seats right behind Spike Lee.

Both my grandmother and mother thought New York was a crazy city. I remember driving once through Manhattan with both of them in my car, I was weaving in and out between taxicabs, and they were in the back seat looking out with eyes as big as quarters. I was used to driving in the city and just going with the flow of traffic, but they both said, "John, get us out of here."

Playing in a city like New York, the melting pot of society, opened my eyes up to a lot of things. But people are people, no matter where you are. People are the same wherever you go. I told people back in Tulsa who asked me about New York that New York was just like Tulsa, but there's just more of it. More people, more buildings, more crime. They would ask me if I was scared being there and I'd say, "No, because I treat everyone the same." I treated Donald Trump the same as I did the guy who parked my car in the garage under the Garden.

I loved New York. I loved its energy and being in that mix. When I came home to Tulsa every summer, I would be going 100 miles per hour. My grandmother would look at me and say, "Son, you need to stop and smell the roses." But I didn't know what she was talking about at the time. Except I'd come over her house and stay maybe ten to 20 minutes before I'd be back out the door. Before I experienced New York, I'd pay her visits and stay at her house for an hour or two.

"Boy," she'd say to me, "you're just on the go."

Even though I lived in Stamford, Connecticut, just coming into New York City to play at the Garden, and sometimes hanging out afterwards, I got caught up in the rat race. Once I was up in Harlem getting my hair cut and this guy started yelling at me for shooting two for 18 in Game 7. It was crazy. That's why I loved going back to Tulsa in the summers. It gave me a feeling of peace.

A lot started happening for me in 1994. Barry Sanders, who had attended Oklahoma State, and I invested in the black-owned American State Bank. I also signed a four-year endorsement contract with Adidas, and in the contract Adidas agreed to give me $10,000 so I could build a new court at my old elementary school, Burroughs. The old court was made out of gravel and dirt, but when the new court was built, we had a big ceremony there.

That summer I started the John Starks Foundation in Tulsa. I wanted to give back to underprivileged teenagers who wanted to attend college, but didn't have the means. So the charity was set up to award college scholarships to 10 selected high school seniors each year and provide them with contacts for jobs during the summers and after college. In ten years now, we've awarded college scholarships to 100 different young men and women. I'm a giving person, and I wanted to pick and choose whom I gave to. I had examined my heart, and I knew that helping people achieve their dreams in life would be so fulfilling to them and to me.

I particularly wanted to help my youngest brother Ju Ju get control of his life. The accident he had that crushed his foot in the oil pump had taken away his athleticism. He had been a cocky kid, always talking about his brothers, but the accident had sent him into an emotional tailspin and the surgery had gotten him hooked on morphine, which led to his cocaine addiction. When my mother had moved the family out to Sacramento when I was in college, Ju Ju got caught up in the gang life out there and continued it when they moved back to Tulsa.

One day near the end of the summer when I was due to go back to New York, I went out driving on the streets of North Tulsa looking for Ju Ju. I always thought that if I missed seeing him before I went back, I might not ever see him again. It was raining hard out and I saw him on a street corner and picked him up. I told him that I couldn't understand why he was living the way he was because he didn't have to. Seeing him obviously high and dazed made me start to cry. Ju Ju just broke down too then, and started crying. We both just sat in the car for a while crying.

He said later that at that moment, for the first time, he saw how his addiction and lifestyle were affecting me. He told me, "I know it's terrible on my wife and two kids, but I didn't realize it was affecting you so much." But he still wasn't ready to change. Less than six months later, he stabbed a man in his side during a robbery attempt and was sentenced to 13 years in prison on an assault with a deadly weapon charge.

The first time I talked to him as an incarcerated man, he told me, "A lot of people ask me in here why I'm doing drugs and gang-banging when my brother, John Starks, is a millionaire. I tell them, 'Because John Starks chose to live his life and I chose to live my life.'"

I began receiving calls from Monty telling me that he thought I was getting lazy, that I wasn't working out as hard as I used to in the summer. He kept telling me that in order for me to become a superstar, I couldn't lose my work ethic. Monty was afraid that I was too giving and that I had to stop helping people in Tulsa, even my own family, and start thinking more of myself. But that's not me. I couldn't stop thinking of how close I once was to following the paths of Monty and Ju Ju. My two brothers were in prison and I asked myself, "Why them and not me?" I thought about that all the time and I still do.

Destiny comes down to decisions and choices you make at crucial junctures in your life, and I realized I could have easily made the choice not to pursue my dream of playing college basketball. Monty quit playing football at Northeastern State University to come back to Tulsa and live the street life. He didn't know at the time that there was something more out there for him. I came close, too, when I came back to Tulsa after getting kicked out of Northern Oklahoma, to just hanging out with my buddies and smoking weed every day, selling weed to get by.

Monty made his choice. There wasn't a whole lot of opportunity for him, and he liked partying and he couldn't let go of Tulsa to find something different for himself than the life he already knew. But if he had gone in a different direction, his life could've opened up for him. Prison life didn't break Monty, but it almost killed him.

Prison life ended up saving Ju Ju. It was a blessing for him because he was at wit's end, so tired of living the gang and drug life. On April 30, 1995, while in prison, Ju Ju accepted Christ into his life and he went through a drastic personal change. The experience purged all the hatred out of him. When he got out on parole three years later in 1998, he gave up dealing and doing drugs and being a gangster and he became a tool for God!

"I'm not ashamed of the type of life I led," he told me, "because it led me to God, and now He's using it for his Glory. Prison saved my life and my soul." Probably the proudest moment in my life was seeing Lawrence straighten himself out and get back on track. It was inspirational for me.

CHAPTER 19

EXORCISING GAME 7 DEMONS

"How can you tell John Starks not to play wild? That's what makes him good."

—Doc Rivers, a teammate of Starks's

I felt driven to atone for Game 7 of the NBA Finals. I wanted to get back to another Game 7 so I could erase the previous one from my mind. I wanted more than anything to bring a championship to the city. One New York newspaper's sports pages started calling me, "The City's Adopted Son," because of how fans identified with my aggressive style of play. One headline read, "Blue-Collar City, Blue-Collar Guy." Little kids would come up to me and pound their chests and say, "I got heart like you, John Starks."

Jeff Van Gundy, who I had become close to because he visited me in Tulsa every summer and helped me work on my game, said to me, "John, you understand New York fans. You're one of the few guys who really understands the mentality of where they come from."

What I like most about New York fans is that the people are up front. If they like you they show it, and if they dislike you, they show it. I respect that about the people in New York. Players who come and play in New York have to understand that here you take the good with the bad. I always took the good with the bad without any complaints, and I think the fans sensed that.

I thrived on the enthusiasm and the energy the fans brought to the Garden. When the crowd got going, oh, man, that was the most exciting feeling I ever felt. I loved playing in the Garden, feeling the pressure mounting and all of a sudden stepping up and knocking down a big shot. I would hear the roar of the crowd and I'd feel energy shoot through my body. There was no other feeling like it. I would backpedal downcourt with my shooting hand still hanging in the air. That excitement is why I wanted so badly to win the Garden fans a championship.

I started the season in an awful shooting slump. Besides two games early in the season against the Jazz and the Lakers, when I scored 35 and 23 points, respectively, I did not score more than 20 points in any other of our first 24 games of the season, and we staggered to a 12-12 record. I was shooting 37 percent from the field, 30 percent on threes and averaging just 12.8 points per game.

One of the problems was that the league had moved the three-point arc in from 23'9 to 22 feet, and I fell in love with the three. I always liked shooting the three. I set an NBA record in the Finals for shooting the most three-point shots in a seven-game series (50), and I'm second behind Derek Harper for making the most threes in a seven-game series (16). I also hadn't recovered fully from my knee injury, so my explosiveness to the basket was still limited, and then with the three-point arc moved in, it looked like a much easier shot to make.

During the 1994-95 season, I shot more than ten three-point shots in 15 different games. In 1993-94, I had shot more than ten threes in only four games. The 611 threes I took for the season, an NBA record at the time, is 161 more than any other Knick has ever taken during a season, Allan Houston's 450 in 2002-03 is next on the list. I made 217 of them, also an NBA record at the time. Allan again is next on the Knicks' three-point shots made list for a season, after my 150 treys in 1996-97, with 148.

Some people thought the reason that I was slumping in 1994-95 was because I'd just signed a $13.1 million, four-year contract extension. Dave Checketts, the Knicks president, the man who signed me to the deal, even said, "I just hope that what we did didn't make him lose his hunger. Because his hunger is what made him an All-Star."

But I was making $800,000 my All-Star year, the 26th lowest salary of the 27 starting shooting guards in the league, and I didn't let that bother me or affect my game. I always say money is off-court stuff and will take care of itself over a career. I know myself. I know what drives me, and money doesn't drive me. I know that I have to have it to live, but money is not my sole purpose for being on earth. Money is not a driving factor to me, and it never was. When I stepped out on the court, whether I was getting paid $1 or $1 million, it didn't matter to me. I was out there to perform. I was brought up by my mother and grandmother to work hard regardless of what I was being paid. I worked hard at the Safeway when I earned $3.35 per hour.

Now watching the game from a coach's perspective, I see some NBA players go out on the court and not give 100 percent, and I wonder what is going through their minds. Some players let the money determine whether they're going to be competitive or not. But those of us who are very competitive don't let money be the determining factor. We're going to go out there and play hard no matter what. Those are the guys I want on my team and in my foxhole.

It's become a problem now with players going out and playing to pad their statistics rather than trying to win. They feel putting up big numbers will lead to a big contract. That's why it's hard for a team with young players to win, because a lot of them think, "If I have a big year in my contract year, I'm going to get capped out." They're thinking of themselves rather than what they can do to make their team win.

Take today's Chicago Bulls team, for instance. They've got a lot of talent, but all of their young guys want to be superstars and get the big contract, so they're more concerned with their numbers than they are with winning. They have all the talent in the world, but they still can't win. The Los Angeles Clippers' talented young players knew they weren't going to get paid by their ownership so they put up big numbers so they could get paid by another team. The only time the Clippers were a decent team in the last decade or so was when Larry Brown was their coach for 1 1/2 years back in 1992-93. But Larry knew how hard it was going to be to make that franchise a winner because the owner wouldn't spend money. Now Donald Sterling finally realizes that he has to pay to keep some of those young players. But think of all the No. 1 draft choices they had coming in over the past 15 years and they still couldn't win. It was ridiculous.

In a game against Atlanta on December 9, 1994, eerily exactly nine months to the day since I hurt my knee in Atlanta the previous season, I played so poorly that after the game I said to the press that I was going to ask Coach Riley not to start me in the following game against Philadelphia. I didn't actually say anything to Riles, but not only did he not start me the next game, he benched Greg Anthony and myself for the entire game. Riles didn't like his players to advise him on how he should coach.

When it came to a shooting slump, I always thought the next shot was going to be the shot that broke me out of it. The next one will get me off, and I'll hit three or four in a row, and

I'll be back in my rhythm, and everything will be like it was. I was always searching for perfection in my game. When I wasn't shooting the ball well, I tended to put a lot of pressure on myself to get it together.

But this time I was so frustrated. Doc Rivers said it was the first time he'd ever seen me hesitant to shoot since he'd been playing with me. I'd been in shooting slumps before, but never this bad and for this long. I knew I'd come out of it, but I didn't know when. I believed it was only a matter of time, because I was putting in a lot of work on my shot in practice and I knew that work would eventually pay off. I'd always seen my work pay off in the past. I'd always been able to work my way out of trouble. I could always get hot again.

The press started criticizing me for the shots I took. I knew they were tough shots. Sometimes they were shots outside the context of the offense. But they were shots I could make. I had to believe my shots were going to start falling.

Coach defended me, saying, "If you want to rake him over the coals, rake him over the coals. The guy's had too many big minutes for us, and we're trying to change a few things to get him into the rhythm, but he cannot buy a bucket. We know he's got a big heart, plays hard. We know he wants to win. He is pure about those things, and that's the way it is."

On December 14, six months after Houston, Game 7, I decided to watch the tape of that game. My thinking had been, "Why watch it? How can it help?" But mired in my slump, I realized then that I had to watch it to get it out of my mind. If you run away from something for so long, it catches up to you and that's what had happened to me. I had been trying to put it out of my mind by not thinking of it, but I couldn't do it. I hadn't wanted to let it overpower my life. So I finally looked at the tape of Game 7 so that I could get it out of my system and so that it would keep me driven and motivated.

The next night, in Sacramento against the Kings, one of my favorite places and teams to play against, I broke out for 19 points in a win. Then on January 6, in a home game against the Cavaliers, another one of my favorite teams to play against (I always played better when I went up against ex-teammates like Mitch Richmond and Tony Campbell), I started a stretch of 19 games where I scored 20 or more points 14 times. The team went on a 15-2 winning streak around that same time.

A partially dislocated left shoulder sidelined me for one game, but the team and I finished strong. We won 55 games, our fourth season in a row with at least 50 wins, to finish second to Orlando in the Eastern Conference and I averaged 15.3 points per game, second again only to Patrick on the team. But the game from that season that most people remember is the one where Michael Jordan scorched me for 55 points in only his third game back from his first retirement.

When Michael came back that first time, there was a big difference in his game. His timing was off, but miraculously he seemed to get it back in that one game at the Garden on March 2. The game before he came to the Garden, I saw him on TV hit the game-winning shot against Atlanta and I said to myself, "Oh, my Lord, he's pumped up now." I knew it was our misfortune that he was playing us next.

Phil Jackson always like to give me a dig, so after the game, when Michael had not only scored 55 points, but passed off to Bill Wennington for a game-winning layup in the final seconds to win the game, he said that it looked like I'd forgotten how to play Michael. That was part true, but it was also true that I was excited to see him back playing. Before I ever became a professional basketball player I was a fan of Michael's. In that game at the Garden, he got on a roll, and no matter what I did defensively, he was hitting shots all over the court. The next time we faced the Bulls in April, I played him a lot better. He scored only 28 points on eight-for-19 shooting.

I believe that there will never be another player as great as Michael Jordan or have the same effect on the game that he did. He played on such a high level, and his magnitude was amazing. Everyone wanted to be like Mike. He could beat you in so many ways and the few times when I felt I might have the upper hand on him, he'd flip my advantage to his own. There's no other player who ever came close to him in talent, willpower and the ability to win. Magic Johnson and Larry Bird were similar players in those areas, but they were not quite as dominant as Michael.

Kobe is a great player, but I think his problem is that his teammates don't trust him to play at the same level that Michael attained. Michael's teammates had the utmost trust in him and, just as importantly, they respected him. I don't think Kobe has that same level of respect from his teammates. I think the Lakers and Phil Jackson trust Shaq more than Kobe, because when Shaq goes down the Lakers are a .500 team.

Another thing about Michael that was so special is how sound a fundamental basketball player he was. He was like Tim Duncan. He did everything so smoothly and simple, but always with flair, too. Because he was so explosive, people overlooked his footwork, his ability to always be in the right spot on the court and his shooting form. He made the game look so easy, even at 40 years old.

Lebron is a fascinating player. I didn't realize how good he was when I watched him playing in high school against guys not really as talented or as big as he is. But he's doing the same thing in the pros at 18 and 19 years old that he did in high school and that's amazing. When he gets a jump shot down—which he's working hard on—he's going to be devastating. The things I love most about him are that he has a work ethic and a sense of his deficiencies as a player. That's what you look for in a young player. He has his own expectations and he doesn't let other people put their expectations on him. Also, he probably has an open line to Michael's cell phone, so whatever questions he needs answered he's getting them solved by the best.

We beat the Cavaliers in four games in the first round, and then Reggie and the Pacers came into the Garden for Game 1 of the Eastern Conference Semifinals. If we were still smarting over Game 3 of the Houston series the previous year when Cassell knocked down that big three at the end, Game 1 against Indiana was even worse. We thought the game was over, and then Reggie made two incredible plays.

We held a six-point lead with 18.7 seconds left when Reggie scored the last eight points of the game and we lost by two. Reggie hit the first three off an inbounds pass with my hand right in his face. On the second, he stole Mase's inbounds pass when Greg fell down with a little nudge from Reggie and he stepped back behind the arc and nailed it.

With the score tied 105 and 13.2 seconds left, I went to the line and missed both foul shots. My mind was rushing. It was a hectic last few seconds and I should've backed off the line and gathered myself before I shot those free throws. I couldn't believe what Reggie had done.

Reggie got the rebound off my second missed free throw and was fouled by Mase and hit both foul shots. I had had a pretty good game up to then, scoring 21 points and making the only two free throws I'd taken in the game just a minute earlier, but I missed the two free-throws that meant the most at the end. It's as simple as that. I took the blame for that loss. I had to put it on my shoulders.

Coach Riley said, "We played our hearts out to get the win and simply gave it away."

Larry Brown said, "We stole this one."

Reggie said, "The Knicks are choke artists."

But that game is a chief example of why I can never understand why reporters write that when a team is blowing out another team, the winning coach should let up on the other team. You never know when the losing team might stage a miraculous comeback and as a coach, you don't want to teach your players to let up on a team. If you're blowing a team out, you want to tell your players to keep pouring it on because you want to put it in the other team's mind that you have dominance over them. That's how you develop the mental edge. If we had won Game 1 decisively, there's a good chance we might have had an easy series with Indiana.

In Game 2, I outplayed Reggie, scoring 19 points to his ten and holding him to three for 10 from the field and we won by 19 points.

We lost Game 3 in Indiana 97-95 and then got blown out in Game 4. Back in the Garden we won a squeaker, and then we had to travel back to Indiana for another possible Game 6 elimination in Indiana. The Market Square Arena crowd got on us real good. Spike Lee was terrified of that crowd. He needed an escort to get down to his seat. But he predicted a win.

Spike said, "We're going to win this series. I'll be in Indiana at 7 p.m. on Friday wearing a John Starks jersey. And I'm going to talk to Reggie the whole game."

The Indiana crowd sure didn't like it that for two years running we knocked off the Pacers on their home court. Patrick had a big game with 29 points and 14 rebounds.

Riles said after the game, "We've got a wild bunch, a great wild bunch."

If Game 7 against Indiana in 1994 was the greatest win I ever experienced, Game 7 against Indiana in 1995 was right up there with one of the worst losses I ever experienced. We were down 74-59 in the third quarter and rallied to close the gap to only two points with only seconds remaining. The Garden was rocking. Patrick got the ball at the free-throw line with his back to the basket. He looked toward me out on the wing, spun left and drove right past Derrick McKey and went up in the lane for a two-foot, right-handed finger roll. The ball hit the back rim and fell off.

Coach said afterward, "He just didn't get it to fall. This team had two great two-year runs. We tried to do it again, but we just did not achieve it."

It was disheartening because we would've gone up against Orlando in the Eastern Conference Finals, and I saw it as my chance to get back to the Finals and redeem myself. We had played well against Orlando during the regular season even though we had dropped three out of five games. It would've been a good series. I think the league really wanted to see us go back to the Finals against the Rockets as a rematch of the '94 Finals. Rivalries make for good basketball.

Riles turned down a five-year, $15 million offer from the Knicks, and instead went down to Miami to be the Heat's coach, president and part owner. They were offering him $40 million and full control, so you do the math. The Knicks weren't going to give him that kind of a deal.

Riles was a very intuitive coach and he knew his players well. He knew his style of coaching wore us down. He's not oblivious to how hard he works his players. He knew what he had to do to motivate us and get us to perform best under his system. He was ready to move on. He had pushed us as far as he could push us, and he felt that he might have lost us. I think he thought he had gotten everything out of us that he could. We'd played in 68 play-off games over four years, against the best teams in the league, the Bulls, the Rockets and the Pacers, and if not for a bounce here and a bounce there, a tipped shot, we could've won an NBA championship, possibly two.

Phil Jackson couldn't help but give Riles and the Knicks one last dig after the Indiana loss.

"It just seems to me that they've put together a group of guys who are not terribly skilled," he said. "The Knicks are pre-dictable. Their offense is run on execution and not creativity. Any time you do that, you're going to get rigid in tight spots."

It was hard to argue with a guy who'd won three championships as a coach and had Michael Jordan and Scottie Pippen on his side. There's some validity to what he said. We did put a lot of pressure on ourselves because we were not a fast-break team. The way we ran our offensive sets, it was always going to be bang-bang. Whether we went inside to Patrick or ran the pick-and-roll with Patrick and me or went inside-outside, our timing had to be just right. But that was Riles's system. No one went off on their own. Phil Jackson's triangle offense keeps you moving. But his offense is all about execution, too. If you don't run the triangle right, you're not going to get a good shot.

It's easy to criticize when you have two of the NBA's 50 greatest players on one of your teams, then four future Hall of Famers on your other team. Riles understood what type of team we were and he put us in the system that best suited our abilities. That is the mark of a great coach, understanding his personnel.

CHAPTER 20

NELSON NIGHTMARE REDUX

"Don't worry about Nelson, John. You'll still be a Knick long after he's gone."

—A Knicks fan calling out to Starks as he
walked out of the Garden after a game

I had turned 30 during the summer, and even though I had had my worst year in three years the previous season, I felt strong coming into training camp. The Knicks had hired Don Nelson to succeed Riley, and I felt it was funny how paths cross in the game of basketball. I began my career with him and we had not seen eye to eye, but now that we were reunited on the Knicks and I was a much better and more mature player, I was willing to let bygones be bygones.

I felt I could revert back to my aggressive style of play, taking the ball to the basket more, because I was a full year past my knee surgery and I was feeling much better. I planned on relying much less on the three-point shot. I was actually looking forward to Nelson's open-court game.

But mentally, I don't think Don Nelson was ready to come to New York and do the job that was required coaching in New York. There is an intensity required when coaching the Knicks that Nelson, with his experience in Milwaukee and San Francisco, didn't have. Nelson was also not used to coaching superstars. The only true superstar he coached before Patrick was Chris Webber, and he insulted and alienated him. We'd been schooled by the best in Coach Riley and were a veteran team, and Nelson wasn't ready to take over our kind of team. If Riley's practices were wars, Nelson's were tea parties.

Nellie's really not a practice guy. He pretty much rolled the balls out to play and then you go home. No drills, no breaking down plays, you just play. But he lost us that way, because under Riley we were used to working hard in practice. Riles had instilled his work ethic in our team so we knew what it took to win. With Nelson as the coach, we knew we weren't working hard enough.

Then Nelson coming into New York right after the Chris Webber situation made it more difficult. His contract negotiation with Webber had gone bad. Webber had signed a contract that he could opt out of if he chose to do so. He had been the Rookie of the Year in 1994, so he opted out of the contract he signed with Don Nelson thinking he'd get a better deal. Webber and Nellie started having words and Nelson tried to turn the veteran players on the Warriors against Webber, saying, "I can't pay you because I have to pay this rookie." Nelson thought everyone would be on his side, especially when Webber left at the end of the year to go to Washington, but the fans hated Nelson after that.

Don Nelson jumped out of the pan and into the fire coming to New York. He tried to come in and overhaul a team that had won 223 regular season games over the past four seasons—more wins than any other Knick teams over a four-year period (the championship teams of 1969-73 won 217)—and reduce both mine and Patrick's roles. It wasn't like we had big free agent players coming onto the team like we did the following year when we won 57 games again. The only two new players were Charlie Ward, who was a rookie, and Doug Christie, who at the time had played a total of 90 NBA games.

We started the season hot with a 20-7 record, but then we went 16-19 for the next 35 games with a five-game losing streak at the end of February that ended Nelson's days as the coach of the New York Knicks. After averaging 15.6 points per game for the first 20 games of the season, my minutes and point production dropped severely. I scored in single digits in 23 out of the next 39 games and played less than 40 minutes per game in every one of those games except one. My scoring average dropped to 11.8 points per game by the time Nelson got fired.

I had tried to forget the past when Nelson came over to coach the Knicks, but our relationship deteriorated when in December, Coach Riley returned to the Garden for the first time as coach of the Heat, and I hugged him before the game. Right after that, Nelson started playing mind games with me, like taking me out of games I was doing well in and putting me into games but not running plays for me.

I started getting very frustrated. On February 5 in a loss at Indiana, I kicked a chair on the sidelines when Nelson took me out of the game after only playing 29 minutes. The next day, Thomas Hill, a young reporter for *The New York Post*, called my 74-year-old grandmother, my mother and my two sisters, who were all working at the John Starks Sports Café in Tulsa, and asked them about my feelings on playing for Don Nelson.

I thought Hill had gone way over the line. You don't call a 74-year-old woman and ask her about what's happening with the Knicks, especially without asking my permission first. I know I could've have shown my contempt for what Hill had done in a better way than walking up to him after practice the next day and threatening to kick his ass like I did. But I wanted to tell him exactly what I felt. If you want to know what is going on, ask me. Don't go behind my back to find out what is going on with me.

Hill got Callie West, a 74-year-old woman, fuming over the situation. "He doesn't have to tell me," she said of me in the article. "I can see it on his face. It's the coach's fault." She said she was going to come see me play in Dallas against the Mavericks in late March and if she saw Nelson, she was going to "tell him to his face." That's Callie West for you, never afraid to tell someone what she thought, but I still didn't like Hill getting her upset.

Reporters have their jobs to do and I respect what they do. But my family is off limits. A lot of the other reporters came over to me after the incident and said that Hill had gone too far by calling my family without my consent. It wasn't like he was going to uncover a new scoop by talking to my family. They knew I was frustrated and upset with Nelson, but they knew less about the Knicks being 1,500 miles away in Tulsa than most Knicks fans did. I always got along well with the reporters who covered the Knicks, but I had to respond to that article and from then on I stopped reading the New York sports pages.

In a stretch of 14 games from the middle of January to late February, I averaged a little over half a game of playing time. In late February, after a home loss to Atlanta where I scored 26 points on 10-for-18 shooting, Nelson replaced me in the starting lineup with Hubert Davis and we proceeded to lose the next four games. Then he tried to trade me even up to San Antonio for Vinny Del Negro.

I was fuming. Everybody thought Nelson would be a good coach with the Knicks, but sometimes nightmares happen. I was driving to the basket and doing what he asked of me, but it didn't make a difference. Finally, after practice one day, I went into his office, and had a talk with Nelson, but it turned into a screaming match. He ended up saying that Hubert's just a better player than me, and that I should get used to that. And after that, I just walked out of the office. I just had to block it out and play in the same way I blocked out 20,000 fans when playing in an opponent's arena.

What Nelson said to me about Hubert being a better player than me didn't hurt me. I knew by then what he was all about. I knew he was just taking jabs at me for being in the NBA. He had tried to blackball me from the league by calling me "too wild" and cutting me, but I had worked hard to overcome the odds against me. I know that upset him and this was his way of trying to take me down again.

I looked at it like this: I don't let a man make or break me. No man can control my life; only God can control my life. What Nelson felt like he was trying to do, it was in God's hands. When the Knicks fired Nelson and replaced him with Jeff Van Gundy, I felt like I was given a new life with the Knicks.

Nelson is the kind of coach who holds grudges. I think he still held a grudge against me for confronting him as a rookie player at Golden State over playing time. Seven years later, I think he still remembered that. I respect coaches like Nelson and I take them for who they are and leave it at that.

I came back from missing a game because of an ankle sprain to score 19 or more points in six of the first eight games under Van Gundy. We respected Jeff because he's a hard worker. Jeff was involved. Even though he didn't have any experience as a player in the league or as a head coach, we knew what we were getting with Jeff. He's a student of the game. The reason he always looked so beat up is that he stayed up long hours overnight watching countless hours of tape preparing for games. He lost a lot of hair working so hard. Give his brother, Stan Van Gundy, the new coach of the Miami Heat, a couple of years working that hard and he'll start to look the same as Jeff.

Jeff's shortness actually worked for him as a coach, because he didn't have to worry about anybody trying to fight him. But he was a tough guy and he'd been a feisty little guard in college. I remember one practice when we didn't have enough players because of injuries to run our drills, Riles told Jeff to jump in. We were running a fast-break drill and Jeff came down the lane with the ball and Oak just crushed him. Jeff got up and screamed, "Oak, you M-F," and Oak just started laughing. I know Riles was chuckling inside, too. It was funny.

Derek Harper noticed the difference in how our style of play changed with Nelson out and Van Gundy in. "The body language with this team out on the floor is different," he said. "Everyone is working together and pulling together now. We're playing with a lot more energy. This team is altogether different."

I was enjoying playing the game again. Mase noticed the difference in me right away and said, "With John, it's an enthusiasm. It may seem crazy on the outside, but it's stuff we need. I like to look over and I like to see some of his excitement because it gets me up, too."

I could never understand when reporters, players and fans criticized or booed players like Mark Jackson and me for showing our emotions out on the court. I like it when players show that they're having fun while they're doing their job. The reason why Mark is still able to play for the Houston Rockets at 39 years old is that he's still enjoying the game.

In the first round of the playoffs, we swept a good Cleveland team—they had won the same amount of games in the regular season as us, 47—in three games. I averaged 19.7 points per game, seven higher than my season average, on 56 percent shooting from the field and 64 percent from downtown, with seven assists per game.

Next up were the Bulls with Dennis Rodman, Ron Harper, Steve Kerr and Luc Longley added to their squad. They had gone 72-10, the best single-season winning percentage in NBA history, and I asked Jeff for the chance to guard Michael more. We had been switching Muer onto Michael and even Derek in recent games, trying to wear him down.

It was a great feeling to go up against Michael because of the challenge. I knew I had some great battles with him in the past and I was looking forward to more to come. I felt I was still one of the best shooting guards in the league. I never lost faith in my skills.

The Bulls, though, were too much for us in that year's play-offs. In Game 3 at the Garden, after losing the first two games in Chicago, I broke out for 30 points, my career playoff high, and we beat the Bulls in overtime, 102-99. But the Bulls knocked us off in five games. They lost only three out of 18 playoff games in winning their fourth NBA title, and we had to go home empty-handed another year. I faced Michael Jordan for the last time in a playoff game on May 14, 1996, and for me it wasn't heaven. Michael scored 35 points while I only scored ten points and the Bulls easily won.

Monty:

I watched as many of John's games as I could in prison and I saw sometimes that John's mind would drift away for some reason. I blame it on the fact he didn't practice as hard as he was supposed to. Once he reached a certain level, he started doing everything people asked him to do. He was too obliging. John's given to Tulsa more than any pro athlete who's ever come out of Tulsa.

He wasn't working out in the summers the way he used to when he would go out and play against anybody at anytime to get his game better. Once he got to that certain level, he knew he was good and he started slacking off a little bit. I'd speak to my grandmother and she'd say, "John so needs you."

In the off season, when John should've been practicing at least two or three hours a day, he took it easy. After I was gone, he didn't have anybody to tell him to get up and go out and work on his gam. I wanted John to get to that Jordan, superstar level.

I'd talk to him before every game and I told him what I thought he needed to do and where his shot selection could've been better. When John started shooting the long ball, I told him to take his game to the inside more. Instead of sitting out there and shooting the three, he should've been taking his butt to the hole. "If you're not making your outside shot, take your butt to the hole and make a couple of lay ups." When John drove to the hole and dunked or made a nice pass, that got his game going. Sometimes he got caught up in that three-point crap and he'd settle. I think I was John's harshest critic. Even when he played well, I saw things that he could improve on.

Monty wasn't around. Monty was locked up. I always put the same effort in as I did when I started off as a player. When I got older, I learned how to work smarter, so I didn't have to work so many hours. When I was a young player, I didn't know how to work efficiently. All I knew how to do was work.

I always worked hard in the summers because I knew Riley's routine. If I didn't come back to preseason camp in shape, I was going to fall behind real quick. After Riles left, I didn't play as much basketball in the summers as before or play in the parks anymore, but I always ran and lifted. What Monty didn't realize is that the NBA season is long, and I had to let my body rest more in the summer to recuperate.

CHAPTER 21

THE COMEBACK KID

"I think that's the most important thing people understand. Never give up on your dreams because of obstacles in front of you. Just continue to hurdle all of them. Just keep going."

—John Starks

A t the end of the 1995-96 season, Dave Checketts called me into his office and asked me, "What guy do you want in here next year, Allan Houston or Latrell Sprewell?" I originally told Dave that I thought Sprewell would be the better guy. I thought because of his toughness he would be a better fit to play in New York. But then I said, "If you can't get Sprewell, Allan will be a great player here, too." There was talk of the possibility of Reggie Miller coming, but I knew Reggie wasn't going to play for the Knicks. He was just trying to drive up the ante for his contract in Indiana.

When it turned out that the Knicks signed Allan, I was very happy. We needed shooters around Patrick and Allan can get his shot up over anyone. Because of his size, 6-6, he could also play the small forward position, too. Dave didn't say that Allan would replace me in the starting lineup, but I knew that there was a strong possibility that I'd have to move into the sixth man role. Sometimes change is good for you. It renews your spirit.

Sometimes you have to adjust as a player in your career, and I knew this was going to be a year of adjustment for me. I don't have a big ego. The Knicks were paying me to go out and play basketball and win ballgames, no matter what position they put me in. I was definitely a different player from the player I was when I made the All-Star team. More than two years after the knee injury, I was still trying to get back the explosiveness that I had. I didn't jump as high as I used to and I didn't have the same lightning-quick first step anymore. I didn't have that hard push to the hoop that I once had. But for the first time since I hurt my knee, I finally felt like I was close to getting back to where I was. I wasn't there yet, but I was getting close.

The Knicks also signed free agent Chris Childs and traded Mase for Larry Johnson. There was talk that Charles Barkley might join the team before the LJ trade and Charles would've been 33, but who doesn't need a Barkley on their team? He would've been tremendous playing in New York, but LJ played well for us. We finally had all the pieces of the puzzle put together: a solid big man in Patrick, muscle, scoring and experience in our other big men, LJ, Oak and Buck Williams, good perimeter shooting with Allan and me, and solid point guard play with Childs and Charlie Ward. In training camp in Charleston, South Carolina, we started wearing shirts and caps with the slogan: "Twelve Men, One Goal."

We broke out of the gate 26-7. Still, Barkley said we had no chance to win a championship and beat the Bulls. "One of their big problems," he said, "is that their best shooting guard is sitting on the bench. I mean, John Starks is tough and he can play."

When Mase returned to the Garden for the first time with the Charlotte Hornets he said, "I'll tell you something, without John in the starting lineup, without his ferociousness and big heart, the Knicks are kind of lost out there. But, hey, that's the politics of the game. The Knicks didn't spend $56 million on Allan Houston not to start him."

I appreciated the kind words from Barkley and Mase, but I disagreed with them over my new role on the team. Over the years, besides not having another good outside shooter, what was missing most was that player who could come off the bench and provide a spark. Mase won the NBA's Sixth Man award in 1995, but he was more of a bruiser and a defensive presence underneath the basket, he didn't put up big scoring numbers. I was scoring nearly 14 points a game, and for the 25-27 minutes I was on the court, I defended the top scorers on the opposing team, the big guards like Michael, Steve Smith, Ray Allen, Jimmy Jackson and Reggie.

Even though I was playing fewer minutes, I was sharper because I knew I wasn't going to be out there as long as in the past so I had to make every minute count. I liked my role, because I got a chance to see what was going on out on the floor before I stepped into the game. I got to see the flow of the game.

We beat the best teams in the Eastern Conference. Five teams that year—the Bulls, Miami, Atlanta, Detroit and Charlotte—besides the Knicks, all had 50-plus win seasons and our record against these teams was 14-7. I was making the big plays at the ends of game. In November against the Raptors, I scored 11 of my 13 points in the fourth quarter, including two steals and coast-to-coast lay ups that ended the third quarter and started the fourth quarter.

In the next game against the Timberwolves, I sank four straight free throws with 20 seconds remaining to secure an 82-79 win. The following game against the Magic, I dived across the floor trying to save a loose ball and the Garden crowd of 19,763 rose to their feet to applaud. I scored 15 points in 22 minutes to spearhead the win.

"That was a huge play, the dive on the floor," Jeff said. "That's the type of play John brings to the game consistently. I think it all starts with him on the defensive end. It always has to my knowledge and always will, that and driving the ball to the basket. Then the jump shot seems to fall more consistently. He's emotional and that's good for us, because at times we don't have enough passion."

I sat out four games in late January with a sprain of my right sterno-clavicular joint, where my collarbone connected to my sternum. I had gotten whacked on my right shoulder, but when I returned, we went on an 18-3 winning streak. Ten days later, Jeff kicked me out of practice and suspended me for an away game against the Milwaukee Bucks because I hadn't gone in for treatment on an off day for a bruised thigh injury I had. We got into a little shouting match in front of some of the guys. I felt I was right, he felt he was right. I didn't look at it as crossing the line. It was more man-to-man stuff; Jeff and I still had a good relationship.

Jeff said that we had a love-hate relationship, but I knew he was about winning, and he knew I was about winning. Sometimes when people are so competitive like that, they kind of cross each other up. We didn't let the disagreement have a long-lasting impact. There was the game later in the season against Indiana where Jeff changed a fourth-quarter play call at the end of a time out and I missed it. When I committed a turnover because I was confused, Jeff and I exchanged words out on the court. But after we won the game, Jeff and I made up in a closed-door meeting in his office.

I owed Jeff a lot for helping me develop as a player, and he owed me, too. Without the success the team had when he was an assistant coach, Jeff probably never would've become the head coach. I know he appreciated me as a player, because after our disagreements, Jeff told me so.

"We've been together eight years," he said. "When you came here you were the fifth guard on the team. You went all the way from the fifth guard to become an All-Star and now you're the league's top sixth man. Factor in the sacrifice you've made for the team in supporting Allan; I don't think in the NBA you see many times where a guy stays on a team and willingly accepts such a change in roles. I think that goes to the heart of how much you want to win and how much of a team guy you are. Your spirit is channeled in the right way. You want to do it for the team."

Chris Childs had fought back from a bout of alcoholism and playing in the minor leagues to earn a major role with the Knicks. Chris and I really clicked playing together. He was signed as a free agent after resurrecting his career by playing five seasons in the CBA with six different teams, and one year in the USBL, before making a name for himself with the Nets. He had come to the Knicks planning on being the starting point guard, but when he saw how well he and I played together, along with the other second-team players, Chris Dudley, Chris Mills, Buck Williams and Terry Cummings, Chris told Jeff he'd prefer to come off the bench, too.

Chris said about the two of us, "We have come basically from unknown to make it, and once we made it we just didn't relax and think everything is going to be simple, we're still working hard because we enjoy playing this game. Once John gets going, I'm always looking for him. And he's going to let me know he's open, too. We've had the same type journey." Charlie and Allan had the same type of personality, they're very low-key, calm people. Chris and I are hyper. So it worked well for everybody.

On February 18, I hit a buzzer-beater at the Garden against Phoenix for a 95-94 victory that sent the Garden crowd into an uproar. In April, I scored 26 points and hit seven threes in a road win against Atlanta, giving the Hawks just their fifth home loss of the year. A three-pointer I hit in a road game against Cleveland with 1:18 left propelled us to a victory. We finished the regular season with a road victory against the Bulls, just their 13th defeat of the season, and we split the season series with them two games all. I scored 20 points in 25 minutes.

For the season we won 57 games, and I averaged 13.8 points per game, playing 26.5 minutes a game, shooting 43 percent from the floor. I was voted the NBA's Sixth Man. We felt we had a great chance to dethrone the Bulls and win a championship. Trent Tucker, the former Knick and Bull, who was friends with both Michael and Patrick, had told Patrick that Michael told him that he thought the Knicks could beat the Bulls in the playoffs.

We swept the Hornets in the first round of the playoffs in three games, and I averaged 14 points a game. We won each game comfortably. We started the next series in Miami since the Heat had won 61 games during the regular season and had home-court advantage, but we beat them in the first game, 88-79. The Heat took the second game, but we returned to the Garden and won Games 3 and 4. I had started the series ice cold, shooting five for 24 in the first three games, but in Game 4 I scored 21 points on nine-for-12 shooting from the field.

Buck Williams told me before the game, "John, it's time for you and me to join the other fellows at the dance."

Riles said, "I know John very well. Once he gets it going, he's hard to contain."

Game 5 in Miami is when all hell broke loose. We were up three games to one with the next game back at the Garden, but then we let our emotions get away from us because of the intense rivalry we had with the Heat. Late in the fourth quarter, with the Heat assured a win, P.J. Brown, their 6-11 forward, flipped Charlie Ward, our 6-1 guard, going for a loose ball and a melee started. I had just come out of the game, so I'd barely stepped off the court when the fight occurred, and I ran back out like I was still in the game.

The NBA has a rule that if a player from the bench steps onto the court during a fight, he is suspended for the next game. Well, we all came out there to defend our teammate. I was the first one out there. Oak and Patrick were suspended for Game 6 and then when we lost that one in a heartbreaking game at the Garden—the Garden crowd was raucous and we held the lead the entire game until relinquishing it in the fourth quarter—LJ and I were suspended for Game 7. We had to watch the game from the hotel in Miami.

I thought it was wrong for the league to suspend Patrick, Oak, LJ and me for Games 6 and 7—P.J. was the only Heat player suspended—and it cost us the Miami series and our chance to face the Bulls again. I think due to the situation—we had just seen one of our teammates flipped off his feet where he could've been seriously hurt; luckily, Charlie is a great athlete, as well as a former football player, so he knew how to fall right—the league should've taken that into consideration and not penalized us so strictly. Everything had happened so fast. I had just come off the court so I was already heated.

Suspending Patrick for one game for just stepping in the direction of the play—he didn't actually come all the way out on the court—was a little crazy. The league definitely could've ruled differently, but because we were the big, bad New York Knicks, they didn't give us a break.

Jeff was a young coach, and the reporters dissecting the incident afterward blamed him because they said he didn't tell us the rule of staying on the bench during an altercation on the court. I'm pretty sure Jeff had told us about the rule during the season, but he might have forgotten to tell us again during the playoffs. I flipped the Miami fans the bird when I walked off the court, which is something I deeply regretted doing afterward. I was frustrated and the fans were giving it to me, but if I were in the same situation again, I would probably run onto the court to help Charlie, but I wouldn't give the finger to the fans.

My mentality at the time was not to take any mess from anybody. But I really regretted doing that in front of all those people, especially when a picture of me flipping the Miami fans off appeared on the back page of the *New York Post*, because it wasn't called for. I wasn't being a professional. I never regretted anything else I did on the court, because it was part of the game, but that wasn't necessary.

After that playoff game, I looked to God for my answers of happiness. After what happened to us as a team, I tried to find inner peace. It wasn't just about the games. I had to find peace in my life. I had all the money, a beautiful home, beautiful cars, a beautiful family, but I wasn't happy inside. I had to find out what was making me unhappy.

Monetary fulfillment was there, but the spiritual fulfillment wasn't there. So I made a commitment to turn my life over to God and let Him guide me from that point on. It's a change that was needed. Every man needs to assess himself, sit down and assess what he has in life. My life was good, but I didn't feel fulfilled.

I believed that things had happened for a reason. I felt it was a calling for me. That God wanted me to live my life in a matter that all people can respect. Some changes were evident. I didn't curse anymore, and I kept myself more in check on the court. It didn't change me as a player. That emotional side of me was always going to be there because God gave me that, too. He gave me all my abilities. It's what I do with the abilities He gave me that determines the quality of my life. People sometimes feel that people who believe in Christ are weak. But it's not that way at all. It's an inner strength that He gives you.

I started my eighth season with the Knicks in 1997 playing the same role as I did the previous season, but I was scoring a little bit more and passing for more assists. I would still get heated.

In one game against Washington I got so upset over a foul call that I started to pull my jersey up over my head, but I gained control and didn't lose it. I knew how to calm myself down. I just turned to Him, said a little prayer, and asked Him to take the pressure off me, and He did it.

When you're an emotional player, things come out that you don't understand. I tried to take that emotional side out of my game and be even-keeled, but that's not how I made it into the NBA, so I had to go back to being John Starks. Sometimes my emotions got away from me like Rasheed Wallace's get away from him. He's a great player, but his emotions get the best of him. That's why as a coach now I want players who have that flair, but also have their emotions under control.

Then on December 20, Patrick broke his wrist, going down with a season-ending injury against the Milwaukee Bucks. We couldn't get on a roll after that. A game in January against the Hawks at the Garden was typical of our problems. I had scored 34 points going head to head with Steve Smith, who had 35 points. Down 89-87, I purposely missed my second free throw and tipped the ball out to Allan behind the three-point arc and he drilled a three to put us up 90-89. With only seconds left on the clock and Allan and I all over Smith, he came down and hit a fall-away jumper to beat us.

Later that month, in a game at the Garden against the Bucks, I scored 32 points in 37 minutes and hit nine for 12 three-pointers, including six for six in the second quarter, almost tying the NBA record of seven for a quarter. But with Patrick not in the middle to intimidate and Glenn Robinson scoring 39 points, we lost again.

My grandmother became very ill with cancer in the spring of 1998, and I struggled on the court during that time. It affected me a great deal. I couldn't get back to Tulsa to see her and I knew I had to block it out the best I could, but a lot of times I couldn't get into that concentrated, competitive mindset and play. Basketball players are taught at a young age how to focus our minds on the game and that the court is our safe haven, but I really struggled.

On the last day in March I missed all eight shots I took against the Spurs in a home loss and then six nights later, I missed all six shots I took in a road loss against the Nets. In the last ten games of the season, I only scored in double figures three times. Jeff and my teammates saw the change in my emotions and so did our opponents. Kendall Gill of the Nets came up to me on the court and said, "I see you're not yourself." Jeff said, "On offense, you're playing too much under control. You haven't taken many shots lately. You've got to get emotional and proactive."

We won only 43 games during the regular season, our lowest win total since 1991, and in the first round of the playoffs we faced off against the Heat in a five-game series. In my eight postseasons with the Knicks we had three main rivalries in the playoffs. We faced the Bulls and the Pacers five times and the Heat three times and of those three teams, the Bulls were the best team by far, followed by the Pacers and the Heat.

But the Heat and the Knicks seemed to clash the most. With Riles and Jeff and Patrick and Mourning all having a history with one another, there was intense competitiveness. Before the 1998 playoffs, Riles called Oak a dirty player, but Oak wasn't dirty and Riles knew that. Oak was just physical. He was an old-fashioned player, if you came down the lane, Oak was going to take your head off. In the playoffs, there was a no lay-up rule and every team had it. Oak was no dirtier than P.J. Brown, but that was Riles's way of trying to get the referees on his side.

The Heat was a strong team built in Pat Riley's mold. They had the strong, big-scoring center in Alonzo, the creative, sharp-shooting point guard in Tim Hardaway, two off-guards who could score in Jamal Mashburn and Voshon Leonard, and then solid, physical, experienced role players like P.J. Brown, Dan Majerle and Isaac Austin.

We lost the first game in Miami convincingly and faced a must-win game on a Sunday afternoon. We were trailing by 14 points with about five minutes left in the second quarter when I hit a long jumper and screamed at the top of my lungs at the Miami Arena rafters. Then Allan and I started trading three-balls. Jeff had told me to guard Hardaway, and I was getting all over him. We closed with a 17-4 run to pull even at 50 at the half.

In the fourth quarter, I shook off a blow to the nose and made a steal and a layup, and then I took a pass from Allan and hit a jumper to put us up 80-74. After two jumpers from Allan, I hit a pull-up baseline jumper to extend our lead to 87-79. At 87-82, Allan penetrated and kicked out to Childs who hit a three to ice the game. I ran over and gave Chris a big bear hug, forgetting about his sore rib cage. When he grimaced and told me to stop hugging him, I told Chris, "Suck it up, it's the playoffs, baby, you've got to be ready for anything."

It felt good to be back.

Buck said to the press after the game, "Longer than any time in the two years I've been here, John has been way down. Guys would say, 'He'll come out of it, he always does.' I was starting to wonder, but he picked a good time to come back."

Harvey Araton in *The New York Times*, wrote about my performance, "There you have it, a vintage performance in a hostile environment on a desperate playoff afternoon, all the reasons why John Starks has been, for almost a decade, the most popular of Knicks.

"There it was in one graphic, propitious exhibition of unmitigated gall, why Starks through the years has gotten away with the head-butting, middle-finger taunting, coach feuding—the recurring trauma of being him. Why Starks, and only Starks, could remain beloved after shooting his team to death in Game 7 of the 1994 championship series.

"We always knew that without him, the Knicks would not have been there in the first place. Rumors of John Starks's career death, as usual, were premature. He remains the microcosm of a team that is pro basketball's 1990's B-movie classic. His is the hand that springs from the grave."

We split the next two games. In Game 4 at the Garden, we rallied to win 90-85, and we had our second melee with the Heat in as many playoff series when LJ and Mourning got into it. Jeff ran out onto the court and grabbed onto Mourning's ankle. I thought he had lost his mind and was going to get himself killed.

In Game 5 in Miami, Jeff started me for only the second time in our last 15 playoff games. I hit on five-of-nine three-pointers and scored 22 points and held Hardaway to 22 points on eight-for-20 shooting. We had a 20-point lead in the third quarter when the Heat went on a 20-3 run and cut our lead to two. But Charlie Ward hit a big three that ignited us, and we won 98-81.

It's funny how the tide turned from one year to the next, one playoff series to the next. There was some bad blood between the two teams with Riles calling Oak a dirty player and Jeff calling Mourning a whiner. I didn't get involved in the name-calling, I just focused on making it tough for Timmy to score. If he was going to get 30 points, it was going to be a hard 30 points. As it was he got 22, but it was a hard 22.

The Pacers beat us in five games in the next series. Game 4 at the Garden was the clincher, as they beat us in overtime, 118-107. I averaged 14 points a game in my last playoff series as a Knick. On January 21, 1999, after the player lockout that cut 32 games from the season, the Knicks traded me back to the Golden State Warriors for Latrell Sprewell.

My son, J.J., had heard the rumors and asked me before the deal was done, "Dad, I got to leave school?" I told him, "Yeah, maybe. I'm not sure." And he looked up at me and said, "But Dad, we've already been out to Golden State."

When the deal was done, I sent personalized letters to every New York newspaper thanking the fans for their support over the years and I heard back from so many people. It was funny. Not in my wildest dreams did I ever think I'd have that much effect on people. A lot of players in the league had crowds cheering for them in college and in high school and everywhere they went, but I never really had that. I was just happy anyone was cheering for me when I got to the NBA.

But I think when you grow—and people see you mature—well, that's insight for people to help them grow and mature. If people in New York took anything from how I played, I hope they remember that when they think they can't get any lower, to hold their head high and walk straight again.

I appreciated the support of the fans and I didn't have any regrets except for one. And that's Game 7 when I wasn't able to perform the way I was capable of performing, I couldn't bring a championship to New York, which is so deserving of one. That's the only thing I regretted, that one game and my performance.

The Knicks had traded Oak to the Toronto Raptors for Marcus Camby and I didn't think that was a good trade. You've got to have someone on your team to go out there and do the dirty work. The Knicks went for youth, but I felt at the time that they had sacrificed good, veteran players in Oak and me, and during the playoffs, it's the veteran players who know how to win. I thought that if they were going to make changes, it shouldn't have been core players they traded away. But I told Patrick that I hoped they would go ahead and be successful and win a championship, and they did make it back to the Finals.

I returned to the Garden that May during the first round of the playoffs and watched one of the games against Miami from the tunnel leading to the locker rooms. When the big scoreboard above the court showed my face on its screen, I got a standing ovation that almost brought me to tears. I was touched that the fans missed me. I missed them, too. I missed them a great deal. Once you take a bite out of the Apple, it sticks with you. It's always going to be inside of me. I knew no matter what team I was playing on; in my heart I was still going to be a New York

Knick for life. When they cut me, I would still bleed blue and
orange.

When I reported to the Warriors I was still in shock. It took
a while for the trade to sink in even though I knew the league is
a business. I lived in a hotel in downtown Oakland for the two
months of the shortened-season while Jackie and the kids stayed
back in Stamford. I played in all 50 games of the strike-shortened
regular season and led the team in scoring with a 13.8 average.
My game kind of suited the West Coast style of run-and-gun
play. P.J. Carlesimo loved the energy and emotion I brought to
the team and started me the entire season. P.J. wanted me to be a
leader, a mentor and a teacher to the younger players, which I
liked doing. But I also wanted to win, which we didn't do a lot
of, going 21-29.

The younger players like Antawn Jamison and Donyell
Marshall were amused sometimes by my antics. On one road trip,
they caught me working out in the hotel fitness center at 7:30 in
the morning. I told them it was no big deal, that the room was
open 24 hours. In one game, I got so pumped up I started pounding the "Warriors" logo on my jersey and shouting to my teammates, "We are Warriors! We are Warriors!" In another game I
yelled at them, "You gotta get hyped! You gotta have heart!"

P.J. was still learning the pro game after coming from Seton
Hall University, and I didn't think he fully understood the pro
game. I sensed that as a veteran player I knew more about the pro
game than he did. And when a player knows more than the
coach, that's not a good situation. While P.J. was still learning the
pro game on the court, off the court he was the best person you
would want to meet. He left what happened on the court, on the
court, and didn't take home any personal grudges. You could get
all up in his face over something that happened during a game,
but after a game if he saw you eating out, he'd pick up the check.

It was amazing how he would do that. I never played for a
coach who would fraternize with his players the way P.J. did. I've

got the utmost respect for P.J. His problem as a coach at that time was that he tried to bring his college coaching style to the pros. Coaching in college is more confrontational. In the pros, you're not going to get anything accomplished if you're confrontational, because the players are making more money than you are. In college, the players are hanging on your every word because they're trying to get to the next level. They know the NBA scouts come in and talk with the coaches and the coaches tell them, "This guy's a good guy. This guy's a bad guy." The college kids have to listen.

In the pros it's not like that. The players are standing on their own two feet. College coaches have to learn when they make the transition to the pros that they can't scream and holler anymore. If they do, it becomes 12 guys against the coach, and management is not going to fire 12 guys, they're going to fire the coach. P.J. had a hard time with that. He should've been an assistant coach first and sat back and learned the NBA game. I think at this time in his career he is ready to guide a team because of the experience he has received over the years as an assistant coach.

Coaches can control the college game, but they can't control the pro game. In the NBA, the players win games. That's why Phil Jackson devises the system, gets the players he likes, and then just sits down and shuts up and lets the players play. Calling every play from the bench doesn't work in the NBA. Sitting on the bench as an assistant coach in San Antonio now, I think P.J. probably has a different perspective.

When I played for the Utah Jazz in my last two years in the NBA, 2000-2002, Jerry Sloan would get in your face. He is one tough guy. He's a reasonable guy, but if you got on his bad side, he's from the old school, and he'll freeze you out. He'd sit you down on the bench and not say a word to you. And you'd just sit there until you went up to Jerry and said, "What's wrong, Coach?" Then he'd tell you what's wrong. After you talked to him, then he'd start playing you again, but you had to come to him first. He was not going to come to you. I respect that and I learned a lot from Coach Sloan.

In 2000, the Warriors had traded me to the Bulls for Larry Hughes in a three-team trade with the 76ers also involved, but I only ended up playing four games for Chicago. I didn't want to play on that Bulls team because I knew that mentally, they had given up. After playing on so many good and successful teams with the Knicks, I didn't want any part of playing for a team that was so undermanned. The only reason Jerry Krause traded for me was that I was in the last year of my contract and they wanted to cut my contract from their payroll the next season.

I ended up not playing at all the last part of the 2000 season because the league wouldn't let the Bulls waive the remainder of my $4 million salary. I was willing to give up the last $900,000 owed me so that I could sign with either the Knicks or the Heat, both teams had expressed an interest in me, for a playoff run. I was 34 years old and had played 11 years in the league at that point and I wanted a shot at winning a championship. When I was with the Warriors, Gary St. Jean had promised me that he would trade me to a contending team before the trading deadline in late February, but a deal couldn't be worked out.

The Bulls' two young, promising players at the time, Elton Brand and Ron Artest were sad to see me leave. Elton said, "He definitely helped and showed some veteran leadership, and gave us some good advice. Every practice, every game, he said something new that would help with my game."

Ron said, "He was really helpful to me. We're not that good so he probably didn't want to play for us. It was probably my fault, maybe if we won some games, you never know, he might have wanted to stay."

Playing for the Jazz were my two toughest years in pro ball. At 35 and then 36 years old, I still had a lot left in me, but I didn't get to unleash it. It was kind of nice living in Utah. There wasn't much to do, but it was real family oriented. In the evenings, couples would stroll down the street, hand in hand, taking nice walks with the mountains and serenity surrounding them.

My first season in Utah, I came into their camp in the best shape I've ever been in. I had a great preseason and I thought, "This is going to be fun." Utah was the best deal I had as a free agent and I jumped on it. But it turned out to be a bad situation for me. The Jazz was so stuck in their ways, the way they played the game was set and it wasn't going to change. I grew to respect John Stockton's game immensely; he's a real floor general. I already respected Karl Malone's game from back when he played in the Pig's Pop-Off tournaments in Tulsa. I didn't try to fight their system even though I was an afterthought in it. I just played my two years out. We went to the playoffs once, losing to the Dallas Mavericks in the first round of the 2001 Western Conference Playoffs in five games. In the final postseason game of my career, my 98th playoff game, I scored seven points in 17 minutes against the Sacramento Kings in 2002.

I had my last serious injury of my career while playing for the Jazz. One of my testicles was removed. It got turned on me and I had to have it surgically removed. A reporter asked me about it after the procedure was done, and I lightheartedly said, "Thank God for giving me two." But not being able to play my game, with the same level of intensity as I had displayed throughout my NBA career, was frustrating. My role was reduced and that was hard to swallow. I finally lost my enthusiasm for playing the game that I loved since I was a kid.

CHAPTER 22

WHEN THE CHEERING STOPS

"I want to see John's reaction the first time someone comes down and jacks up a three in transition. John's going to go nuts and I'm going to be laughing."

—Jeff Van Gundy, Westchester Wildfire
season-ticket holder

My Grandmother, Callie West, died on July 5, 1998, of cancer, and then my oldest sister, Anita Peoples, died of breast cancer the following year at age 31. In 2001, my mother, Irene Starks, also succumbed to breast cancer at the age of 58. It hurt losing three people I truly loved one after the other. I just understood that God has a hold of them now and that I had to deal with it. I miss them all a great deal. I remember the night my mother died we were playing a game in Utah and I was sitting on the bench when I felt her spirit leave. I knew then something was wrong. So after the game I called home and got the news that she had passed.

My grandmother had lived with the cancer the longest and she handled it very well. She didn't want people worrying about her. That's just the way she was. It was tough times. I called back from New York to Tulsa frequently and the family would give me reports on her condition. I was surprised when I went to her funeral and saw how many people were there. I knew my grandmother was loved, but until I entered that packed church in Tulsa, I didn't realize how loved she was by so many people. It was standing room only. She had an effect on so many people in our community through her work and her presence.

Ju Ju got out of prison in 1998 and he's a preacher and a caretaker now, working for a company in Tulsa that helps people with assisted living. He helps a man who is mentally impaired get through his day, assisting him in the morning as he gets ready to go to work and then in the evening, helping him prepare dinner and live a satisfying home life. Monty got out of prison in 2000 and he came right out to see me in San Francisco where I was playing for the Warriors.

Monty:

I got out of jail on February 10, 2000 and the All-Star game was being played in Oakland on February 11. I got out of jail one day and the next morning I was on a plane heading to the All-Star Game. I'd been in jail for 12 years and nine months. John sent a limousine to come get my girlfriend, who's now my wife, and me at the airport. In the hotel, all the NBA players were walking around. And then I saw Allen Iverson. Hell, I could identify with Allen Iverson. He'd been in the penitentiary, too.

John told me, "Tell him you're my brother. He'll take a picture with you. He won't say anything.

So I walked up to Allen Iverson and I said, "Hey man, I just got out of lockup. I'd like to take a picture with you."

Allen was like, "Sure dog. Man, you're big."

I was huge from working out with the weights in jail. I told Allen that all the people in jail identified with him and he said, "Why's that?"

"Because you've been in lockup," I told him. "You're one of us."

I got a slew of pictures with Allen and Isiah Thomas and everyone. The next morning I woke up in the hotel bed and I still didn't know if I was in the penitentiary and dreaming or if I was really out. The first couple of weeks were like a fantasy, waking up with no bars around me.

Most prisoners who have been locked up in the penitentiary for a long time and finally get released, they don't get where they went long unless they meditate about their lives. Meditation is good for you. It clears your head and gives you the chance to see what's going on around you. The prisoners who don't get it are the guys who when they get back on the outside, wake up to the same madness every day. They go through a day, lay their heads down to go to sleep, and wake up and keep going. They never sit down and think.

Monty was going from the time he was five-years-old until he hit the prison wall. When he came out of prison, his mind had to change. If it hadn't changed, he wasn't going to make it in this world. I have an extra house on my property in South Tulsa, so when Monty got out of prison I let him stay there. He has his own house in Shawnee, Oklahoma, but Monty's work brings him into Tulsa a lot. He operates his own landscaping company and he's very successful. Rather than having him travel back and forth, I have him stay with me. His son, Brian, is a senior at Langston University, and when he graduates this spring he'll be the second person in our family to graduate from college, after my uncle Curtis.

I don't hide from my son, J.J., what happened to his uncles with drugs. It's part of his life, and Jackie and I have talked to him about it. I tell him that as young men, you often seek wild times and you have to get through those wild times. I've seen people who are very wild and crazy as kids become very productive citizens as adults. I've told J.J. that it's those people who are cautious, like I was, who are able to get through those wild times intact. I like that a lot about my son right now. He's careful about what he does. He thinks things through before he acts.

My oldest brother, Tony, works for Nordam Airlines Supplies, and my sister, Nikki, works for Omni Airlines. My Uncle Curtis is still a physical education teacher and coach at a middle school here in Tulsa. Everyone knows Coach West. A lot of people still come up to me today and say, "I know your uncle, Coach West." He's very well respected and liked in the community.

My brother closest in age to me, Lynn, or "Bucky" as we call him, he's one year younger than me, is not sure what he wants to do in life right now. He's confused. It's frustrating that I can't help him. Sometimes I stress over what I can do for him and that's not good for my immediate family, my wife and kids. It's kind of like a couple of years ago when I retired and had to let go of playing basketball and that was difficult for me, now I just have to let go of helping Bucky. I have to learn to let go and understand that it's his life. He's around in Tulsa, but he keeps his distance from the family. He does his own thing, works wherever he can get a job. Bucky's always been different. Ever since he was a kid and he walked away from that football game, he's liked keeping to himself.

For the past two years, I've worked at my foundation here helping local teenagers find direction in their lives. Helping others, especially young people, makes me feel good. In April, I received the 100 Black Man Award in Tulsa as acknowledgement of my community service in working with youngsters. I examined my heart and felt that giving back was something very important to me.

I've also had the chance the last couple of years to be around my family more. Playing pro basketball puts a lot of stress on your family, especially if you have kids like I do. I was looking forward to retiring so I could go to their games.

My son, J.J., is now 17 years old and has his own dreams of playing in the NBA. He's 6-3 and just finished his junior year at Victory Christian High School, and I'm coaching him now. At times, he shows spurts of greatness. Jackie had been trying to get me to coach J.J. for the longest time. I tried to work with him when he was in the eighth grade, but he wouldn't listen then to what I told him. So I told Jackie that I wasn't going to work with J.J. again until he came to me.

He's the type of kid you have to let go at his own pace, and when he's ready, he'll open up to you. It hurt me to sit back and watch him go through his struggles, but he had to learn like everybody else. He only came back to me last year. But he knew when he came to me what to expect. These days are hell for him right now.

He didn't have to go through the tough times that I went through growing up. I'm trying to put the toughness in him that I learned from playing on the streets. But he's nothing like me. J.J.'s calm and implacable. He reminds me of Charlie Ward, killing them softly. I tell J.J. it's good he's like that; it'll serve him well later in life. But I also tell him that he needs to be dunking with ease. He wants to attend Oklahoma State and play ball for them. He can dunk off of one leg now, but I've told him he needs to be able to dunk off of two legs.

I think it's good that he has the goal to play in the NBA. He's been around the game his entire life. I remember when he was a little kid shooting his little basketball at his little goal we'd bought for him when he was two years old. I'd watch his form, and he had perfect form—it's like his shot now. He shoots the same way he did when he was two, kind of like Tiger Woods's swing. At two years old, J.J. was hitting all net. I was playing for Golden State at the time and I'd come home and play with him and think, "The kid has great form." I guess he used to watch me on TV. Jackie used to sit him up to watch the games and he'd say, "That's Daddy on TV." I think that's how he developed his shot.

I go to every one of his high school games and usually my family members will come, too. I don't know if it's a distraction to J.J. to have me in the stands watching him. He probably wishes I would shut up sometimes, but he needs the advice and for me stay on top of him right now. I'll call him over while he's playing to tell him to push the ball up the court, to take the ball hard to the basket, not to rush his shot if a defender's crowding him, but to pump fake up once and then go around him. I'm helping out his high school coach to be part of his growth as a player. J.J.'s got a laid-back personality, and by me staying on top of him, he's going to break through and pick up his game. His personality is the same as mine off the court, but he needs to understand that you have to flip that switch during the game. That's when he will become a great player.

Growing up, I thought my only ticket out of Tulsa was playing basketball, but J.J.'s got more options than I had, and I'm happy about that. My oldest daughter, Chelsea, is 12 and she is an equestrian, as well as a basketball player. My youngest daughter, Tiara, is three, and she doesn't let anyone do anything for her. "I'll do it! I'll do it!" she's always screaming. Girls are much harder to raise than boys. They're real independent. Tiara is smart as a whip. She turns the computer on by herself and runs the little mouse. If you turn off the TV when she's watching, she throws a fit.

I've had a lot more time to work on my golf game in retirement. I'm now an eight-handicap and I get very competitive when I play. I love golf because it's a mental game. I love things that challenge my mind. I run a charity golf tournament every

September at different golf courses in Westchester County. Last year, we played at Donald Trump's course in Briarcliff, New York, and the money we raised went to my foundation and the Westchester Children's Hospital. I've also taken up playing the saxophone. I've always loved listening to jazz and R&B. One of my favorite songs is Maze's "Joy and Pain."

Basketball is still a big part of my life. Two years ago, I got a call from Gary Lieberman, who is the new owner of the Westchester Wildfire of the USBL, saying he wanted me to be his coach. I had come to New York last spring to attend Patrick's number-raising ceremony at the Garden, and during a television interview that night I said I was interested in getting into coaching. Gary saw the interview and called me up the next day.

Gary is a longtime Knicks season-ticket holder and he knew me indirectly because his friend's mother was a huge fan of mine, and when she was dying of cancer, her son had called my agent and said he'd pay me a lot of money if I came out to visit his mother at her New Jersey home just to cheer her up. I refused to take any payment, but I went out to visit Gary's friend's mother. I was already at the mother's home, when Gary's friend arrived. He entered the house to find his mother and me sitting on a sofa in her living room, his mother's arm draped around my shoulder as she cheered me up because the Knicks had just traded me to Golden State.

My ultimate goal is to coach in the NBA. But I don't want to seek any NBA coaching jobs until J.J. graduates from high school next year. I don't want to move him in his senior year of high school. I think that being a head coach in the minor leagues is better preparation for my future than working as an NBA assistant coach. I already know the NBA game and I'm getting the chance to make executive decisions now.

I like it that I'm joining my old Knick teammates, Patrick, Doc Rivers and Herb Williams as recent coaching converts. Having been coached by guys like Riles, Sloan and Nelson, I think coaching got into my blood. When you have mentors like that, naturally you tend to think about coaching yourself. And the more I thought about it, the more attractive it seemed to me. My teammates were always teasing me when I played, anyway, telling me I'd make a good coach. That's because I was always telling them where to go on the floor and what to do once they got there.

A large part of coaching an NBA team is being able to motivate your players. The USBL calls itself "The League of Opportunity," because it has sent 135 players into the NBA, including Mase, Chris Childs, Charlie Ward, Michael Adams, Darrell Armstrong and Darvin Ham. It's an opportunity for me, too. Eric Musselman, who's coaching the Warriors now, coached in the USBL, as did Kareem Abdul-Jabbar, a person I deeply respect. Right now there are several coaches in the USBL who played in the NBA, including Darryl Dawkins, Robert Reid and Cliff Levingston.

I tell my players to look at guys like Raja Bell playing for the Jazz now. He's not a big-time scorer, but he's a solid player who shoots 45-50 percent from the floor, can knock down threes and can defend. More than anything, I tell my players that the NBA wants guys who can play consistently. If you're scoring 35 points a game in the USBL, but you're shooting only 30 percent, a scout can tell right away that you're taking all the shots. The player doesn't get any assists or steals; all he can do is shoot. But still he scratches his head and says, "Why don't I get picked up?"

Vonteego Cummings, who was my teammate on the Warriors, played on my Wildfire team the last two years and I was shocked that the NBA teams haven't really taken a hard look at him. Vonteego has all the tools. He plays with flair, is a heck of a defender, good ball handler, improved shooter and he is a competitor. He wants to win.

Kevin Freeman is another player who was on the Wildfire two years ago who I felt was overlooked by NBA teams. He knows how to win from playing his college ball at the University of Connecticut, and he's a very talented player inside who worked so hard on his outside shooting that he was the USBL's leading three-point shooter percentage-wise that season.

NBA scouts put guys in boxes. I don't look at numbers. I want guys on my team who are winners; who are going to dive on the floor and defend and do the little things to help us win. The guys who are constantly improving are the guys I want to take.

Look at a player like Mario Elie. He didn't get to the league until he was 29 years old. He stayed active and was determined to play at the next level and he ended up winning three championships on two different teams. He wasn't the most gifted player, but he had an attitude of winning. He won championships in the CBA, the WBL and in the NBA, so he knows how to win.

I try to teach my players how to be professionals, just like Coach Riley taught me. Too many players in the USBL think that as long as they have the talent, they can make it into the NBA. But I tell them talent will get them far on the playgrounds and possibly in high school and college ball, but to play in the pros they have to know how to compete and win.

A big part of my job is evaluating players and telling them what their strengths and weaknesses are, because NBA general managers come to me and other minor-league coaches first, to hear what we have to say on a prospect that they're interested in. I have to give them my honest opinion. I don't want to blow up a player who's really not that good. I try not to do that because as a coach, my word is my most important credential in this league.

I do see a little of myself in these guys. When Kevin Freeman told me, "We all know the struggles you had to get to the NBA. You're a living, breathing example to all of us trying to make it that it can happen." It moved me. The hardest part about being a coach is to cut a player like I had to with Richard Dumas last season because of his knees, who was my college teammate at Oklahoma State in 1988. You're basically telling someone he's not good enough to stay with you and that's very hard.

As a coach who used to play, when you haven't given the game up and start thinking of yourself as a player and wishing you could go into the game and do things on the court, you get in trouble. I'm in a teaching phase now. Teaching guys how to compete and be players at the next level. I emphasize to them the importance of playing defense. Defense wins games. I try not to make too many changes, even though in our 30-game season our team's roster is constantly changing due to players coming back from playing overseas and college kids joining the team.

Two seasons ago, Kwan Johnson, a 6-3 guard, came onto our team in the middle of the season and he had been the MVP of the league the year before. In his first two games with us, he was the leading scorer in both games, but I still brought him off the bench rather than disrupt the chemistry of the team and start him. One thing I learned from Riles is that you don't change things unless you must.

I know that these guys are really still kids when I see them get excited by the Golden Arches. I tell them on game day to take a nap, stay off their feet and cell phones and spend some time during the day just relaxing and meditating on who they're guarding that night and what they have to do to stop him. Game day is about shutting down everything and getting ready to play. It might be tough because we might have been on a long bus trip from Dodge, Kansas to Salina, Kansas, but if I don't mind it, they shouldn't either. I don't mind sopping sweat off the gym floor or driving in a bus. I'm an ol' country boy. I've never been spoiled in my life.

I have a son who's going to go to college next year and a daughter who's going to be driving in a few years so I'm getting old, but I'm not so much older than some of my players on the Wildfire that I can't relate to them. I have the people's touch. I think I'm pretty good at talking to people and I try to translate my passion for the game to my players.

I can get along with anybody. I don't care what a person's background is. It's just my personality. I'm outgoing and I treat everyone the same. I treat Donald Trump the same as the man on the street who doesn't have anything. It doesn't make a difference to me.

People who meet me now and get to know me often say, "Man, I can't believe you're the same John Starks I used to see playing for the Knicks on TV." When it comes to competition, I know how to hit that switch inside me that says, "It's time for me to win," even if it's only playing a game of golf with my friends. I always know how to turn that switch off when I'm not competing. When I played, it was like I was an actor, playing a role, playing a character. I wasn't that same character when I stepped off the court, just like the actor playing a murderer killing people in a movie isn't that same person when he leaves the film set. People got so attached to me as the basketball player who sometimes acted wildly on the court that they can't believe it when they see me off the court as a nice, caring man who helps children.

What I miss most about playing is the playoffs. That is the only time of the year now where I start wishing I could play again. That is the time I miss the most. Talk to any NBA player and they'll tell you that 82 games is a long stretch to try to keep yourself in shape and stay focused. But the energy level that surrounds the game during the playoffs—the fans, your focus, the do-or-die situations—the intensity makes those games a lot more fun to play.

I worked this past year as a pregame and halftime analyst for Madison Square Garden Networks, who broadcasts the Knicks' games. When I was a young player and would hear interviews of mine on radio or TV, I didn't think my voice came across clearly so I took speech lessons. Now I practice my speech by going into my study and reading the newspaper out loud. Before I go on air for the live segments with Al Trautwig, it's just like when I stepped out on the court, I build myself up to be more exciting. I tell myself it's "game time." I don't do any verbal warm-up exercises. I just go on and tell the viewers what I see.

I think the Knicks are heading in the right direction. I don't know if they're going to win a championship in the next couple of years, but if Isiah continues to make the right moves, they could contend. Isiah's gotten the team younger at the point guard and small-forward positions, with Stephon Marbury and Tim Thomas, and at center with Nazr Muhammad. The team has got to shore up its defense and that might be tough, because most of the players are offensive-minded.

I think about the course of my life a lot and how I could have very easily followed the path both Monty and Ju Ju went down. I think about that all the time. I watched drugs destroy my brothers' lives when they were still teenagers. I could've easily gotten caught up into the drug and crime life. I think it is the Grace of God that He sometimes picks one kid out of hard times and lifts that person up as an example to the others that there is another way. That if you work hard and keep the faith, you can succeed and not fall prey to drugs and the street life. I've been fortunate and my family has been fortunate. Monty and Lawrence have turned their lives around when they could've easily been killed.

I think back to that two-year period that Monty and I had together when he helped me develop my game and I won scholarships to Oklahoma Junior College and then Oklahoma State. I think about that time often. I think God gave Monty a chance to do good before he sent him on his way. God gave him an opportunity to do something right. God gave Monty one good deed to do.

It's like God said, "You're out here messing up and destroying my children selling dope. I'm going to give you one good deed to do before I take my hands off you and let the world have its way with you."

Monty should really still be in prison. He really was supposed to do more years. He only got a 13-year sentence, but he could've gotten 25 years to life for robbery with a handgun, even if it only was a b.b. gun. I tell him, "You thank God. He blessed you by allowing you to enjoy life now and have an appreciation for living in this world."

I know Monty likes to think that he made me into the person I am today. That he instilled his will, his strength into me. We argue about this all the time. I know I had that strength in me already from growing up watching my mother get beat up by so many men and getting beaten myself by both Monty and Tony. It created a deep river of anger in me, and that anger sometimes came out when I got heated playing basketball. When I got ticked off on the court, that's when I got the best out of me. I watched my mother closely, what she went through, the trials and tribulations, and I saw the heart that she displayed. She didn't want any of her children to fall into the same traps that she did. I learned my mother's survival skills.

As my mother got older, she thought more deeply about her life. She wasn't ashamed of her past. But she finally came to a point in her life where she was really happy. Monty didn't get a chance to be around her when she got over everything she went through and found the Lord and became a more soul-searching person, because he was still in prison. Monty thought only of what she put him through without thinking of what she went through. My mother was a very talented interior decorator and used to advise people on how to decorate their homes. I tried to get her to go to school for interior decorating, but she wouldn't go.

Near the end of her life, many people sought my mother out for counseling. She had a sobering effect on a lot of people. She'd been through so much so she knew a lot. What she had seen through her eyes! People respected her so much because she told them exactly like it is. She didn't beat around the bush. If you didn't want to hear the truth, you didn't ask her any questions because she was going to let you know.

Monty:

To me, it's kind of like John and I are attached at the hip. I came home from prison and John has got this house on his property with nobody staying in it, and he wanted me to stay in it. He and I have this close bond for what we've been through together, and it's not the same with our other brothers and sisters. John and I can be cussing each other out one minute and then 30 minutes later, we'll go out to play golf with each other. It's just like that.

We argue all the time. On the golf course, we sometimes get into crazy arguments that start on hole 1 and end at hole 18. We communicate by arguing. We don't even root for the same teams. John goes for Oklahoma State and I go for OU. John goes for the Steelers. I go for the Raiders. We can argue over anything, but we've got this real solid bond. I can't imagine that ever changing.

Every July 4th, we have a barbecue at my house and then we all drive back to Elwood Street in North Tulsa and set fireworks off outside my grandmother's house. It's a tradition. The whole family is there, as well as many of our friends, the kids who grew up with us in the old neighborhood, and we all get the chance to see each other again. My cousin, Antonio, lives in my grandmother's old house now. Tony, Monty, Bucky, Ju Ju, Nikki, my uncle Curtis, and all our families gather and talk about my grandmother and mother, Anita, and everything we have to be thankful for today.

My mother always said, "Don't ever, ever give up. Keep going forward. Don't let anyone destroy your dreams." And I've always strived to follow my mother's advice. My wife sometimes says to me that I should try to find my father, but I'm not interested. I always had a big, close family around me, and that was enough growing up and it's enough now.

People ask me now that I'm a coach how I would've coached John Starks, the player. And I tell them I would let myself shoot all the time. No, I'm just kidding, but I let players be themselves. Whatever gets an individual going, let him get on a roll, that's good by me. As long as what he's doing is helping out the team.

I'm a coach now, but I still think about playing all the time. The game will always be in my blood. It's a game that I love. The Dunk comes up in my mind and I can still see it play out just like it was yesterday. Then I start thinking about Game 7. It is always with me, too. Going through a game like that, it'll never leave me. Anybody's who's ever gone through a night like I had in Houston and who tells you that they've forgotten it, don't believe it. They're just telling you a story.

But I never got caught up in that whole fame deal. I miss the game, but I don't miss all the hoopla surrounding it. I stay grounded. I don't get ahead of myself. I live day by day. I just take what each day brings. I never was a big superstar when I was young so I don't let things go to my head. I just treat people as people with respect and the way that I want to be treated. I don't need 20,000 fans cheering me on a daily basis.

The story of my life is about surviving and never giving up on my dreams. I've been through a lot, but my whole family has been through a lot in our lives. When I got kicked out of junior college and came back to Tulsa to live with Monty, I knew I was moving in the wrong direction. One day I decided to get down on my knees and pray to God to take me and my family out of the situation we were in. My grandmother always taught us that if you don't have any answers, to get down on your knees and pray. Two years later, I was in the NBA.

I prayed and I dreamed and I followed my mother's philosophy on life. She'd say, "Live day by day. Don't get too far ahead of yourself". None of us back then could really see any further than what we saw on any particular day. My mother could have been put in jail for a long time for shooting Nicole's dad when I was only seven. My brothers Monty and Ju Ju could still be in jail to this day. But living day to day helped us to get through the hard times and I don't live any differently today. I still follow what I heard my mother say time and again, "You don't know what's going to happen to you tomorrow so enjoy the day."

JOHN STARKS'S BEST, BIGGEST AND FIERCEST TEAMS

Best Team
Michael Jordan, Magic Johnson—backcourt
Larry Bird, Charles Barkley—forwards
Patrick Ewing—center

People might argue with me over the center and power forward positions, but I knew what Patrick stood for when he took the court. He was going to give it everything he had. He was a presence in the middle. Hakeem was great, too, but I'd take Patrick over him and David Robinson. I respect Karl Malone a lot, but I have to give Barkley his due. He was only 6-5, but he was a monster underneath.

Fiercest Competitors
Michael Jordan
Reggie Miller
Joe Dumars
Isiah Thomas
Vernon Maxwell

Best Shooters
Michael Jordan
Reggie Miller
Mitch Richmond
Joe Dumars
Byron Scott

Biggest Gunners
Michael Jordan
Reggie Miller
Mitch Richmond
Patrick Ewing
Vernon Maxwell

Best Minor-Leaguers to Play in the NBA
Anthony Mason
Tony Campbell
Mario Elie
Darrell Armstrong
Michael Adams
Muggsy Bogues